Left Turn, Life Unimagined

Jen Eikenhorst

Published by Jen Eikenhorst, 2022.

While every precaution has been taken in the preparation of this book, the publisher assumes no responsibility for errors or omissions, or for damages resulting from the use of the information contained herein.

LEFT TURN, LIFE UNIMAGINED

First edition. May 5, 2022.

Copyright © 2022 Jen Eikenhorst.

Written by Jen Eikenhorst.

Table of Contents

Introduction 1
Prologue. 7
Big shoulders. 10
Atypical-Tuesday. 14
The last memory. 17
Plans changed. 21
The unimaginable. 26
The hardest call. 29
Love is, knowing. 32
Complicated case. 37
Every little detail. 44
Facing the hill. 51
It doesn't look good. 57
Unanswered prayers. 62
Am I a killer? 67
In it, together. 70
Love abounds. 74
Divine appointments. 80
Facing the mirror. 87
I'm fine, I lied. 90
A memorial for David 93
Left turns. 95
A time to mourn. 100
No coincidences. 105
Free consultations. 112
Love is persistent. 116
Sleep past the pain. 122
Love unconditional. 128
The power of prayer. 135
The least of these. 138
Brooklynn's story. 140

Baby steps.	142
More steps.	147
Searching for community.	153
Pray for them.	157
Hard conversations.	166
The elephant in the room.	172
Something unexpected.	175
Crumble or crack, panic attack.	179
Breaking point.	185
Sermon illustrations.	188
Series of firsts.	193
Feeling sentimental.	198
Countdown to Grand Jury.	203
Equipped.	208
Saving grace.	213
Dear David,	215
Salvation	219
Afterword	221
Acknowledgement	223

For Chris, you are and always will be my life-love. Patrick, Katy, Logan, and Haven, I love you. Thank you for being a reason I never gave up. For Mom & Dad who loved, supported, and believed in my healing, no words can express how blessed I am to have you both. For the beautiful souls that supported us, helped edit this book and a million selfless acts, thank you. For the community that shares this heartbreak, we are never alone. Never lose hope.

Left Turn, life unimagined

• • • •

COPYRIGHT © 2022 JEN Eikenhorst All rights reserved

This book is a memoir. It reflects the author's perception of experiences over time. The names, characteristics, and places have been changed. Some events have been compressed, and some dialogue has been recreated.

No part of this book may be reproduced, or stored in a retrieval system, or transmitted in any form or by any means, electronic, mechanical, photocopying, recording, or otherwise, without express written permission of the publisher.

All Scripture quotations, unless otherwise indicated, are taken from the Holy Bible, New International Version®, NIV®. Copyright ©1973, 1978, 1984, 2011 by Biblica, Inc.™ Used by permission of Zondervan. All rights reserved worldwide. www.zondervan.com[1]. The "NIV" and "New International Version" are trademarks registered in the United States Patent and Trademark Office by Biblica, Inc.™

• • • •

COVER DESIGN BY: STEPHANIE Snyder

---

1. http://www.zondervan.com

Epigraph

••••

OPEN LETTER FOR THE grieving (accidental death):

    I am so very sorry for your loss. If the person that hurt your family member never shared their sorrow openly with you, I do. There are no words that feel big enough to express regret for your pain and suffering. I wish there was a reasonable answer to why these accidents happen. I pray you have found the strength needed to endure this loss, the comfort to heal your broken heart, and the peace that surpasses all understanding. I also pray for you to experience what God wants for everyone– the abundance of life and fullness of joy while honoring your grief. We can only trust God that in this circumstance we all experience the miracle of his healing. I pray you have found forgiveness because the courage to forgive sets you free. May you find the beauty amongst the ashes of grief and may the love you shared cover your broken heart.

    Deepest condolences,
    C.A.D.I.

Introduction

Could you live with yourself if you accidentally caused an innocent person's death? More people than I care to recount have point blank looked me in the eyes and said, "I don't know if I could live with myself." I live on by the grace of God, and I do so in awe because of a man named Jesus. I knew I loved this person from Bible stories when I was a little girl; everyone told me how much he loved me. I don't know how I knew he was real, but I knew him. His name was not spoken in our home, but I would sing made-up songs from my heart to him. I would find him in the joy of dancing around my room, talking to him about my day. I would ride my bike and find him in the clear blue skies and the sweet breeze. I was gifted my first paperback Bible at age ten from church camp. During the middle school years, I would regurgitate stories I had heard but probably got all the characters mixed up.

I would paraphrase scriptures with maybe more commentary than the written Word. I didn't know exactly where to find it hidden in the chapters, but I heard its truth, and it stuck in my heart. This was the reality of a baby Christ-follower from a non-religious home. I testify to the bus ministry that came to my apartment complex and picked up children for Sunday school. Their service made a difference. It was not perfect, but it was genuine–personal to my core and, in many ways, innocent of the pain of being raised in the not-so-perfect church.

All my life, I've wanted to help people. I prayed for a career that would make a difference. I am living out those prayers in a way that I would have never imagined. I will never believe the Lord orchestrated the events in these pages maliciously. For reasons beyond my understanding, God allows suffering that takes us to the edge of our breaking point. Let me tell you, I reached the splintering phase where cracks began to form in every aspect of my life.

I felt the weight of the pressure when I tried to hold it together in desperation and realized this was beyond me. I broke, and I let God pick up the pieces to restore my soul. To come through this meant accepting that it would not be of my own strength. Surrender is terrifying and beautiful at the same time. God's Word promises he will never forsake me (or you) in the darkest times. After reading my journey, I pray for you to have a new picture of grace and unconditional love. I hope this story invokes hope in all things you may have faced or will someday face, even those that are unimaginable. In October of 2016, I felt I had lost my will to live in an instant; every joyful, moral, and valuable moment leading to this day was gone. Or so I believed for a time.

After my thirty-sixth birthday, I felt every good deed or honorable thing in my life was erased. A death to my identity. I had to start over. My normal would never be again. After the accident, my world suddenly darkened and crushed from what I always believed, that I had a purpose for my life. What kind of purpose was this? Was God good and loving? Things will eventually work out if you are a good person, right? This accident happened to an innocent person and to me. Our truths collided; we were connected in this tragedy. Weren't we both good people? Was I now the villain in my story? I thought this is how it feels to lose hope on several occasions. I had experienced many miracles before the accident, but I never lost hope.

Since that fateful day in October, I have battled a voice that shouts, "You are a monster!" And each day, I remember who God says I am and ask for God's truth to ring louder and the strength to endure. This is my journey of healing after the accident. There is a family not directly mentioned who was first and foremost impacted; this fact should never go unnoticed. I think about them every day and the incredible loss they suffered. I don't know their story, and I acknowledge my sharing may pain them, but I, too, have a voice.

LEFT TURN, LIFE UNIMAGINED

Throughout the Bible, like Daniel 4:2, we, as Christians, have an obligation to share healing, restoration, and hope with the world. I fell short and made a human error. When I say that out loud, "error" doesn't feel like a strong enough descriptor for what I did. Because I failed to yield the right of way, an innocent man lost his life. That's it, done. Nothing I do can change that fact. Everything I ever was became displaced like the fragments of mirror, glass, and metal scattered along a quiet country road. The decision to turn left brought me from an average school teacher to an accidental killer in the blink of an eye. A community of outcasts.

But here I am, a C.A.D.I., meaning, Causing Accidental Death or Injury. My lawyer said, "Jenna, no one cares who you think you are. If we go to trial, we will have other people tell the jury who Jenna Anderson is. People from your school and church, fellow teachers, longtime friends, and your husband will paint a picture of who you are beyond this accident. The jury is more likely to see you clearer through the eyes and stories of people who know you instead of hearing it from you."

I stared back, trying to think if anyone would have anything concerning to say about my character. I snuck out with friends in high school and drove down to Deep Ellum, a somewhat sketchy part of downtown Dallas known for bars. Once there, our thrill was quickly turned to panic. God thought it was a perfect time to teach me a lesson when my dad's '92 Corolla wouldn't start.

It was there next to a spray-painted gang-tagged D-Town Killaz parking garage. I vowed as a sixteen-year-old to never do it again. Or, in the heart of betrayal, I let my temper fly and said the most hurtful hateful things I could think of and called my very best friend since childhood "trash" because I let a boy come between us. I lied about my age at work as a young adult because I was tired of speculations about how I got such a big promotion in sales as a barely twenty-year-old bright-eyed, ambitious personal banker. I was making a mental list of all my wrongdoings when I heard Mr. Strawn abruptly remind me, "You're the offender." His blunt nature and honesty about the road ahead are what I needed. I appreciated that he skipped the sugar-coated BS that most people trying to be "nice," fed me.

The 30-minute consultation certainly shook me up. It was slightly terrifying even though I felt there would be evidence to support an upstanding citizen of moral character. But the possibility that my life as a wife, mom, school teacher, and community member would also include indictment for vehicular manslaughter was simply devastating. Whatever my accomplishments, volunteer hours, or reputation I was once known for were gone moving forward. I was sitting in a criminal defense attorney's office. We had no money for the retainer; I sat there in shock and humiliation. Humbled was an understatement.

I used to make jokes about things like this. What kind of Christian needs a criminal lawyer? Shameful that I once mocked and judged, but I need one now. I need the best Christian Criminal Defense Attorney on this side of Texas, and it is comforting to know they exist. Comforting, yes. The caveat is… good attorneys are like rare coins, expensive, and hard to find. My family was willing to sell everything if it meant my freedom. I knew that legal representation was needed, but I did not feel worthy of being defended. I didn't understand my guilt because I followed the law, and at the same time, I felt the enormous weight of causing this pain.

Voices slithered into my every thought that I was now a killer. You don't deserve love; it should have been you. Who was I after the accident? Nothing felt familiar on my skin. Was I still the mom of four kids? Yes, but I could not care for them; I could barely care for myself. I also felt they were now ashamed of me. Was I still married to my loving husband of 15 years? Yes, but certainly not a "Proverbs 31" wife; I just brought so much shame on our family.

LEFT TURN, LIFE UNIMAGINED

Am I still a firstborn daughter, the strong-willed, independent Jenna Lynn that my parents raised? Yes, but for a time, there was no fight in me, no passion. I was a shell of my former self. I felt part of my soul also died that October night. For many months I wore a mask. This book is the deconstructing of that time six months post-accident. Where was God? Was He good? Where was my faith? Who am I now? I was bound by invisible bars that formed a prison of shame. Anxiety overtook every thought and action, crippling me. I hated myself.

The accident was a pivotal point mid-life, my fork in the road. Would I take the path less traveled towards purpose from pain and fight for healing? I was on a journey to make sense of the trauma, find myself, and find my faith. The glimmer of hope in this story is God's promise that he will never leave us nor forsake us, even in the self-loathing hells we condemn ourselves to. He walks with you there while you are trying to find your way. I have found peace and faith to endure without a typical happy ending. If you are triggered by depression or suicidal ideation, please discuss reading this book with a mental health professional.

Know that there is a turning point. I wrote my truth for my healing, but I pray it helps someone else. I don't want sympathy but compassion for the collective of us that live out this burden. The battle to not be attention-seeking steals your voice and robs you of healing. I exposed my soul, my moral injury, and my deepest and darkest thoughts dwell in these pages with nothing left to hide because 1) We do not just move on with our lives after a fatal accident, 2) We aren't alone, and 3) God uses messy, broken stories for his glory over and over again.

All the names and places have been changed to give some semblance of anonymity for the people I love. I am Jenna, and she is me. It is a name I used once to lie about who I was. At a time in my life, I lost who I was and what I believed in. The name that matters most in this story is the Lord's.

Our names could be interchanged with anyone who has lived through this tragedy. What matters more than names is how the Lord drew near and healed my broken heart. I want to thank all the people in real life that lived this out with us. You know who you are. My perception is my truth, and it may not be as other people view it. I needed a place to hold the heartbreak, hold the memories that felt so close that they took over every thought. Sharing has set me free in some ways. This story is not meant for harm, nor can I expect everyone to fully relate. I pray you take the secret you hold, that thing that brings you shame, and you decide to give it to a Holy God who loves you.

Prologue

Life before the accident was uneventful and routine. That's precisely why I think it's important to share that there was absolutely no significance of the day until the sun went down. Three days before the accident, I was where you could find me nearly every Friday night from August to December for the last 12 years of my marriage, cheering for my husband doing what he loves under the stadium lights. I am there for the team but watching him coach holds my attention. He has overseen every aspect of this sport: offense, defense, and quarterbacks, but secretly deep down in his veins, coaching defense is his favorite. What looks like a patch of 100 yards of well-manicured grass is his mission field. Instead of a pulpit, it's a team huddle where young men take a knee to hear how God is the glory in the win or the loss. I am his biggest fan. I love listening to his highlights of the game and what they will work to improve on before next week. But the best part is to hear the players one by one encourage a teammate to end every game in the huddle. This man I married just a little over fifteen years ago is like that on the field and at home. Loyal, a man of his word. He is a "go-down," with the ship kind of leader if those he is responsible for aren't off the boat yet.

Saturday morning, we were up early with our traditional big breakfast and deep clean-the-house routine. My Grandma Ruby could wake people at the crack of dawn with the call, "biscuits are ready." But the savory smell gave it away; if you were smart you hurried to the table at the sound of the oven door opening. Maybe the secret was the old cast iron pan that was seasoned to perfection that made them taste like magic. Making pancakes on Saturdays was part ritual, part budget-friendly, and part hope for a legacy like Ruby's.

Keith was awake breaking down game film and reviewing the other team's scores from our district while I matched socks from a bottomless bin. You could hear laughter from different parts of the house and dogs barking at the neighbor. The wind blowing in the fall air whistled against the kitchen window and a branch made a screech across the glass in rhythm. I didn't know how blessed I was in these simple moments. The gift of a clear conscience. My thoughts were on grocery store list-making, dinner planning, and contemplating what bin had the fall decorations? I dug out my fall wreath adorned with pumpkins and a burlap bow that said, "Welcome Y'all."

The rest of the day had no more significance than a couple of loads of laundry. Sunday was the kind of morning that shines like I imagine heaven will. Worship, though I can't sing to save my life, is the best part of my week. Music was special that morning as the youth helped lead. Hillsong had a new song that after the first time hearing it you couldn't help but have it on repeat, "What A Beautiful Name." I would hum the chorus for the rest of the day, "What a beautiful name it is, hmm hmm la da da da, the name of Jesus." Lost in the song, my swaying to the melody. Overcome with some emotion thinking about Hazel's recovery from surgery. Over the years I have called on His name over and over because sometimes in life that is the only thing you can muster. Call on Jesus. I worshiped freely that day, hands in the air reaching to heaven. The clapping and rejoicing standing in the presence of the Holy Spirit. I breathed it in. I go back to this place in my mind sometimes, life before the accident.

In the Book of John, Chapter 4, there is a chance encounter with Jesus and the woman at the well. Scholars will tell you this was no coincidence; every move Jesus made was purposeful. Nothing was ever wasted. My moment at the well was coming, a turning point. Somewhere along my journey, I made a left turn, but my encounter with Jesus brought me back on the path that leads to life. Learning to rejoice and trust in things that nearly break you is the greatest lesson of faith and truly the road less traveled. Life after an accident with fatality is one of the most complex human entanglements I can imagine.

Despite the darkest days, there are glimpses of wrong turns made right when we trust God with the journey. Forgiveness does not excuse the circumstance, but it prevents it from destroying your heart. In John 4:13-14, Jesus said, "Everyone who drinks this water will get thirsty again, but whoever drinks the water I give will never thirst—not ever. Indeed, the water I give them will become in them a spring of water welling up to eternal life." In my own walk, I have found this to be true. I am the woman at the well, we are just like her, and Jesus meets us where we are. Thank God for that.

Big shoulders.

Since the age of ten, I have been self-conscious about my broad shoulders. My uncle would tease me about not needing shoulder pads (it was the 90s) or how I would make a great linebacker if I were a boy. Later it would be a joke that if someone would get caught or hurt or unintentionally in trouble...it would inevitably be me. In a sea of zooming cars, I am the one going six miles over that will be pulled over and given the ticket.

These things developed in me a thick skin and a sense of humor. But on October 4, 2016, I unknowingly set my hope, my future, and the happiness of others on fire near the end of a very ordinary day. I watched that future burn to the ground, and I knelt in the ashes helplessly. Amid the devastation and ruin, I believed many lies, including that I was no longer a good person–that I was now unlovable, unforgivable–and questioned why God even placed me on the earth.

Like Job, I cried out my sorrow to the one who controlled my circumstance, the Lord, the only refuge I knew. On a quiet backcountry road, a left turn changed the lives of innocent children and many more when I had an accident with fatality. I was approaching a crossroad at 36 years old; this tragedy could have ended me if I had taken the wrong turn. I lost my way for a time with relentless voices tempting me, but I held on to hope just enough to let God lead.

My heartache was a Jesus-take-the-wheel kind of moment; however, I just wasn't confident it was Jesus who was driving. That left turn took me on a journey to redefine my identity. Every little decision we make sets off a chain of events; the good, the bad, the ugly, and even the tragic all have a purpose. A mosaic, a collection of broken people and shattered expectations, becomes beautiful. A miracle, impossible for human design. But God, the author of our lives, a divine creator, sets things in motion and provides all the support we will need. I can say this is true because I witnessed miracles in everything. The mercies I would need along the journey were already in place. The burden I carry of causing a death never gets any lighter. God allowed the accident to happen. I take full responsibility on my part. Not treating that road like a busy intersection will always be my deepest regret.

I bear all the aftermath with reverence. I won't ever fully understand why, or why him or why me, this side of heaven. I've met with God on the sacred threshing floor and pleaded for mercy and answers. But nothing. Sometimes life can resemble hell, but it's essential to know that this is not our home. Just passing through and everything we go through should help us to see, love, and be more like Jesus. God is the very reason I still breathe. I came face to face with the devil, my demons, and the hell he rained down in a series of spiritual attacks. I survived that; I'm still standing.

In 2016 we had been through so much spiritual warfare; we began to laugh at each new crisis. "What now," we would laugh. Those within proximity of gossip thought we were cursed. No, really, people would ask in the most sincere way, "Have y'all prayed over your house? Repented? Something must be causing these attacks." We, as a family, were still recovering from other challenges that would strain any family. The accident was at the end of a series of unfortunate events such as an unexpected job loss, drastic salary changes for my husband, the death of a former student, and a significant surgery for our youngest to remove a benign cyst. It was an overwhelming year, and we were just halfway through.

We anticipated the next "thing" on alert that the calm was temporary; another storm was brewing just a matter of time before it made landfall. The accident was not just a personal storm; it was a disaster that turned many lives upside down. I honestly wasn't sure we could recover or rebuild from this one. I was tired of having "big shoulders." I was done with comments of our strength for God trusting us with such an "incredible" testimony. Why were we "plagued," I was a fervent prayer-er.

Lord, please protect us while we travel. Go before us with your angels and keep us safe in our coming and going. Let no harm come against us, in the name of Jesus' Amen.

Hundreds, if not thousands, of prayers similar to that effect before every drive would be on my heart and lips for twenty years.

I can't tell you if I prayed for it that night. Was that why it happened? I slipped a ritual with God, and an innocent man lost his life? It doesn't make sense when you say it out loud. Typically, I prayed over every trip. Why not that trip up the road to pick up my daughter? But I know for certain, I never prayed for God to protect others from me, my driving, my shortcomings, my humanness, and I skipped this night. Never did I think I was capable of harming anyone. But I did. I could have never in my wildest imagination, of possible hell storms the enemy would throw at us, would include causing an accident with fatality. I hate that it is written in my life-book. Forever the plight of an accidental killer, connected to the man that tragically lost his life on a backcountry road. The unimaginable.

•••

The world speaks differently than the gentle grace of God. We have to know the difference. Scripture says we will need to know our Shepherd's voice. This can be hard while navigating trauma. Sometimes God calls us to be a voice. I have questioned why I feel led to share something that is so deeply personal, highly emotional, and painfully indicting. My only response is that I feel the Holy Spirit called me to be a witness of God's faithfulness to redeem any situation. He is near to the broken-hearted and he uses the least of these to share his truth. I have asked him to search my heart and motives. Psalm 138:23-24 "Search me, O God, and know my heart;

test me and know my anxious thoughts. See if there is any offensive way in me, and lead me in the way everlasting." I hope that above anything shared you will be inspired to know Jesus as your personal Savior. I hope that you decide to give hope another chance if you have given up.

Atypical-Tuesday.

Our schedules are often dictated by the season. We had a home junior-high volleyball game on the calendar and swim practice for the boys on this particular Tuesday night.

I remember the strangest things, like the weather in detail. If I give a little effort, I can feel it. It would have been a challenge for anyone to complain on a day like this. The sky was clear blue that day. I almost went for a walk at lunch to take in the sunshine. There was a crisp breeze I'd classify as the perfect balance for a fall day. The kind of day that beckoned convertible tops to be down, a reason for windows to be wide open and motorcyclists to ride free. Can't blame anyone for taking advantage of its beauty. With Texas temperamental temps, we never know from one day to the next–like a punch line to our life.

Fall holds a special affection in my heart. I love the turning leaves and pumpkin spice. Our anniversary is September 22nd; I picked it because it is the official first day of fall. We are the couple that practically married straight out of high school. He took me to my prom. Engaged by twenty and married at twenty-one–way too young, but we did it anyway. We were advised against it by friends and family and even our pastor...we did it anyway. Our youthful passion may have brought us together, but the good Lord has kept us together despite the odds stacked against us.

This September, we celebrated fifteen years of marriage. It hasn't been a fairy tale but more of a reality TV series. No big celebration because football in Texas stops for nothing. We spent the milestone in our marriage accompanied by twelve smelly, exhausted, but victorious boys. We considered dinner after a JV game, as a date night. He shared his malt milkshake with me despite saying I didn't want one, and I gave him my extra fries without hesitation. This is our love, comfortable, content, found in small things. Our marriage thus far has beaten the odds for marrying in our early twenties and proved to all those naysayers that it's possible to mean in good times and in bad. We've survived the throes of a multitude of trials. Job losses and career changes, mistakes of various magnitudes, harsh words and insecurities. We practically grew up together as a couple, discovering who we were and what we wanted to do. To make things more complicated we did this and added in the layer of parenthood.

The last six months have been emotionally exhausting, and we were at the breaking point. Teetering in the balance of crying and laughing. Despite the wild and sometimes weird things that have happened in the last decade and a half of marriage, we love the Lord more...we love each other more.

It's the struggles that both build up incredible faith and produce love forged in fire, and we appreciate those lessons eventually. But while we are in the trial it's harder to appreciate how our testimony will help someone else someday. Our family's journey of odd things started on September 11, 2001 (also a Tuesday), while the world watched in horror as the towers were struck. We were unaware and happily applying for our marriage license.

But the accident was on a level all its own as far as trials go. Nothing we had ever faced would prepare us for the heartbreak to come. And in some ways, it is difficult to explain how the tragedy that ultimately affected another family, also happened to us. It doesn't make sense to grieve a stranger, but I wholeheartedly did.

The day was packed. I taught my pre-algebra classes without a care in the world, answered emails about missing homework and pleas for extra credit as we were nearing the end of the first grading term.

God was faithful with my new position this school year. I took a chance and left brick-and-mortar traditional teaching to teach from home. No makeup, messy bun all day, no rushing out the door. I unapologetically taught each day concealing yoga pants and old-lady slippers tucked under my desk and out of view of the webcam. Typically, around this time of year, I start to feel blah and begin an anticipated countdown until Thanksgiving break. But this year was different.

I was exactly where I was supposed to be, relieved even. I had such grand intentions to start working on myself, get healthier, lose weight, and finish up my master's degree. Maybe finish up a couple of book ideas I have tossed around now that I work from home. The irony was that none of that would play out as I imagined.

The day carried on with various sports activities after completing homework leaving a sink full of dinner dishes to finish when we returned from practice. That didn't happen; they were left undone, and I can't recall who washed them or when. Because life abruptly stopped that day. It's interesting how all the trivial moments leading up to eight o'clock are preserved in memory. Maybe this always happens but is never noticed unless something significant like trauma takes place.

My memory of what happened ten-minutes ago is questionable, but I can replay events leading up to the accident like a favorite movie in my mind, preserved as the, "life we had before."

The to-do list I made on October 4th was simple. A list drawn out on a neon yellow post-it was made without the heaviness of depression or guilt. Before the accident I prayed many sweet, soft, safe, fluffy prayers daily but when life gets turned upside down the raw, ugly, begging-pleading prayers for the will to go on come out. And they came spilling out.

The last memory.

My time at the gym with Keith just a few minutes before the accident is a memory I keep in my pocket when life feels too much. This little exchange is like a favorite scene from a classic romantic comedy. The one you save for days you need to laugh or you're feeling down; the one that comes to mind with your besties. You mouth every line and cry on cue and laugh and sob and fall in love with the characters. I still cry when thinking about that moment in the gym, and we never knew the significance.

His whisper near my cheek, lands somewhere between sentimental and euphoric. I can still feel the warmth of his breath, the tickle of his scruff. I love watching our flirtation that evening, cherishing our playful banter like we were twenty-somethings again.

Keith at 6'3" wears an athletic frame with broad shoulders and a narrow waist built like a boxer. He was wearing a ragged navy and gray fire department shirt given to him by his older brother. It's literally falling apart but it's his favorite muscle tee. The edges curl and various size holes expose sun-soaked skin from coaching in Texas heat. And have mercy, his ball cap was on backward which meant he means business with lifting heavy weight.

He walked over to my elliptical like he had something important to say but instead leaned over to check out the stats screen and whispered near my cheek, "Go babe go!" The timer rolled over to 42 minutes. Commotion on TV briefly caught our attention. A home improvement show was playing, a perk of getting a good elliptical. We didn't have cable at home. In front of me are grand windows for soaking up sunsets and people watching. "Honey, you are on a roll" he whispered, the attention translated, "I am proud of you." I smiled and lifted my hair to fan my neck playing it off but giving him a show with my hips and with that, he turned back for the next set.

JEN EIKENHORST

The best part about this machine is its prime location. Good view of the outside straight ahead, nice flatscreen to my right, the weight rack to my left because that's where I can keep an eye on this man of mine. And he loves it too; it's reciprocal.

He made small talk between sets and flashed a smile that showed his dimples. His chin stubble still stirs butterflies like all those years ago when a girl crushed hard on the guy who worked at the shoe store across the mall corridor. That's the same smile he used when shopping at the candy store where I worked as a senior in high school. On his lunch break, he would drop by for chocolate-covered gummy bears. He would spend his 30-minute break listening to me talk and offering to pick up food for me. His chivalry completely stole my heart. Eventually, he also managed to get my phone number, and the rest is history.

He glanced over his shoulder just before a power cling. That sly smile, I knew exactly what his smirk meant. He was flirting, and it was working. We've been married long enough to know what each other is thinking. This is the last happy memory I have had before my accident.

The way he saw me, it was a look that made me feel loved and desired. Worthy of his love. He was physically strong, but at 5'1", I matched him somehow. We fit; we complement. This little exchange back and forth between the weights and my elliptical was magic. We needed this memory; it was something to hold onto as a keepsake. I would soon become broken, lost, and no longer the woman standing before him at the Lake Hills YMCA. The evening should have ended with tucking the kids in bed and then making good use of the playful foreplay from the gym.

That would not be the way it played out. Instead, we lived out a nightmare, and my family lost the "me" they had known for thirty-six years. His family, the victim's family, lost immensely. Three innocent children lost their daddy on that Tuesday. I take responsibility for their grief, their pain, their loss, and how life changed forever for them too. My grief for this reality will never overshadow the fact that I caused their greatest pain.

The plan all day was changed just minutes before life changed of my own doing. Is it funny or cruel how that happens? Irony? Wrong place at the wrong time? Destiny? Twisted fate? I refuse to believe this was God's plan for either of our lives. The man who lost his life, or mine, or his children losing him, or mine almost losing their mom to depression. A tragic web.

God's very nature is to love all in the middle of their mess. He walks us through it, and he is there to help us pick up the pieces. Some of the mess is our own doing, some by other people's choices, some by design—we don't always know which is what. But I know in the mess there is beauty. I cling to that promise. I'm grateful beyond words that I learned that along the way. It was rooted deep in my soul, and it was all I had when everything else felt abandoned.

•••

Romans 8:28 says "And we know that in all things God works for the good for those who love him, who have been called according to his purpose." It is a verse I will doubt for a season; in fact, this was a season I challenged everything I ever believed about faith and the goodness of God but spoiler alert—nothing can separate you from the love of God. I would feel separated for a time. I felt like I was in a season like Job where I would cry out and curse the very day I was born.

But at the same time, I would never regret my life or faith up to this point. Here is where the journey to find my way home begins. Back to the arms of Jesus, fully and completely trust him with the story of my life. My advice in the wake of any tragedy is to hold on to hope for the day. Try to resist looking too far ahead; some things are just too big. Hold on and gather enough strength for that day. And not the strength you think is yours but a supernatural power that comes from a God that does not grow weary. A well that never runs dry, in this tragedy I was not enough, I needed a Savior to see me through it, I still do.

Plans changed.

Love thy neighbor and do no harm are creeds most decent humans live by and when we don't, it changes the soul of a person.

Juggling schedules of four children that have different commitments often sends us racing in opposite directions. The burden to coordinate is typically something I handle. The truth is it takes a village. We carpool and trade out kids with families that have similar ages and joint activities. I am so grateful for my village; they mean even more to me now than they ever did before. Several scriptures come to mind about bearing burdens with one another like in the book of Romans. A friend that is closer than a brother, if you want a glimpse of Jesus, walk with a friend through tragedy and grief. People that are willing to sit in the pit, cry with you, pray with you and just listen, that is the true friendship written about in scriptures. The people God had put in our life, locked arms with us as we faced so many unknowns are treasures. We are forever grateful for their support.

On the day of the accident, we were double-booked. My oldest daughter had a volleyball game that overlapped the boy's swim practice clear across town and Keith would still be in football practice. On days like this, I depend on my fellow moms for help. On this day my friend Terri answered the call to help make it happen. Brooklynn would stay with her best friend Lori to finish up the game, and the boys and I and Hazel would head to the YMCA. Sounds complicated? It was.

Life resembled a juggling act of time, pick-ups, hand-offs, and drop-offs because of the multiple schedules. I'm a glorified taxi driver amongst other duties to keep the Anderson household running. Normally, committing to something new like competitive swimming I would have thrown a fit; however, both my boys were built for it. While they were at practice, I could use the facility. With the stress of job changes and Hazel's medical adventure, I had put on almost twenty pounds. This was my opportunity to commit to myself to work out without mom-guilt. If I had to be there at the gym for the boy's practice and childcare not an issue, I would finally get some "me time."

The plan was that Brooklynn would be brought to me at the YMCA about 8 p.m. after the game and a team taco dinner. I had just reached three miles and I was feeling pretty good about the milestone-a new personal best.

A message from my friend Terri flashed over my cell that she was stopping by the house to drop off her girls to find their chapel stuff and then would bring Brooklynn to me. "We'll be there about 10 minutes later than I thought," she said.

School-uniform life can get crazy, the significance of chapel-eve is when moms across the country panic trying to make sure their children have the designated attire. The night before chapel is an intense scramble when uniforms become the most pressing matter. I have been known to lose my mind over a belt, slip a bad word over a misplaced dress-code specified colored sock, or scream like a banshee because of a perpetually disappearing tie.

"No problem," I replied to the text but then it occurred to me, *it's chapel dress tomorrow.* Dreaded chapel dress. I was out so why should she get back in the cold for my kid? I quickly texted her back, "Hey, don't get back out, I'll come to grab her."

Approximately twelve minutes later, lives changed on that country road. Without a care in the world, I hummed along to some worship songs on the radio to pick up Brooklynn.

If I had stuck to the original plan, maybe things would have turned out different. The enemy was allowed to steal, kill, and destroy that fateful night for reasons beyond my understanding. The man that lost his life had three young children that received the worst news imaginable. They were forced to drop everything and pray they made it to the hospital in time. Ultimately, they said goodbye to their father two days later. But the pain far outstretches just the immediate family. I acknowledge the grief of friends, relatives, coworkers, even the first responders that courageously answered the call to another trauma-inducing accident all because of me.

It was just down the road. I had been there once before but never this time of night. I knew my way by landmarks, not street signs. This subdivision was one of the more prestigious neighborhoods in the area, a gated community of grand custom homes that border the lake.

Brooklynn peered out the arched stone window, ready to dart for the car. Eight o'clock was late for a school night. The days were already shorter, so there was not much visibility beyond the headlights once the sun set. Thankfully, an October cold front chilled the air and encouraged her to not prolong any goodbyes. These tweens will take advantage of small talk if we let them. Her volleyball uniform certainly was unforgiving to the change in Texas temperatures.

"Thanks for feeding her; see y'all tomorrow!" We exchanged waves and made our way home.

"How was the game?" I asked her, reversing from the driveway.

"We lost in the third game." She began to tell me about the details of the game.

I turned the corner and stopped at the first stop sign out of the subdivision.

"Sorry y'all lost, but did you score?"

"No mom, it's a team sport there is no scoring in volleyball, but I got my serve over the net!" She beamed with pride.

I waited for the iron gate to open out of the subdivision.

"That's awesome, sweetie!" I high fived her.

Thump, thump, we drove over the gate grid.

I trickled up to the next stop sign and listened to Brooklynn with enthusiasm catch me up about her serve over the net, the giant burrito she shared with a friend, the homework she needed to finish, and half a dozen other little thoughts that popped in her twelve-year-old mind within minutes of picking her up. When excited she talks even faster and with higher pitch.

She let me know all the things she needed to do when we got home. Find her chapel socks, make her lunch, shower... Hazel made sure to interject her desire to pick out a bedtime story.

Out here on the edge of town there are no road lights. The city taxes stop about half a mile down the road. This stop sign is where the main road leading to town meets the crest of a hill that leads to a scenic lake drive. I looked left towards an old oak, nothing but shadows. I looked to my right and there was nothing but pasture and Brooklynn's mid-thought expression.

No sounds, or motion, or lights; nothing caught my attention. The kind of darkness that soaks up any light like a black-out curtain. This road made me nervous at night because there were a lot of deer. "Watch out for deer," my friend once warned me, terrified of hitting a deer.

I reflect on that thought and my heart breaks a little more each time. Another haunting to sort out.

Glancing to the left again the road was still just as clear as far as my headlights could reach. The old oak was like a soldier standing guard at the gate of Hidden Harbor Estates with proud outstretched limbs. Yet its trunk and branches hid a painful truth; the road was not clear. At approximately 8:01 pm on Tuesday, October 4th I didn't think about the hill or the tree. It was just a tree. I didn't think about looking around for blind spots. I didn't try to understand the bending light around it or what was behind it. Minutes ago I had driven that same climb safely. The evaluation change was not in the slightest of my forethought. The radio was on but turned down so Brooklynn could comfortably talk. No sounds felt out of the ordinary in either direction. It felt like a quiet country road, as it should have been. Just a normal left turn to get home. I did not feel threatened or rushed, just the winding down of an ordinary day. I was wrong.

•••

Psalm 56:8 says that the Lord cares for all our sorrows, he holds all our tears, and they matter. There would soon be buckets and buckets of my tears stored up in heaven. At the moment it's hard to believe complete destruction like that written in Isaiah 61:3, "bestow on them a crown of beauty instead of ashes, the oil of joy instead of mourning, and a garment of praise instead of a spirit of despair." The question is not if trials will come but when. Our relationship with the Lord is what will keep you grounded amid the ruin. God remains the same when everything around you changes. In my heartbreak I have found this to be true, my sins, my choices, other people's sins, and choices are constantly rocking our world. I think I've heard it explained like an orbit. Your relationship with the Lord is the center and things may spin around in your vicinity, but the chaos around you is less cumbersome because you dwell in the secret place of the Lord and that is where you remain.

The unimaginable.

I have many faults and limitations, but I've always been known as an uptight, 10 and 2, defensive driver. Accidents like this weren't supposed to happen to cautious drivers like me. It happens to those, "other people," who are risk-takers, inconsiderate or inexperienced drivers, but not me. I have safely made left-hand turns hundreds, if not thousands of times in my 20 years of driving, and that all changed on Davidson Road. The last thing I saw was a sudden burst of headlight invading our car out of nowhere. Brooklynn's face was caught in the crossfire like a lighthouse spotlight beaming straight in our direction. My hair stood on end. Brooklynn gasped in terror.

I screamed, "That's a car!"

With only a fraction of a second to think, my brain had two choices: slam on the brake or accelerate and hopefully get out of the way. I choose the latter. *I'll always doubt if that was the best choice.* Fear took over, my grip tightened, my elbows locked, and I braced for impact. *Where did that car come from? Is this the last way my sweet Brooklynn would see her mother?* But there was no impact. Instead, there was a subtle bump that if we had not been startled by the light, we might not have questioned the commotion. Whatever happened, it pushed the back end of the car. As it did, we heard a piercing screech I can't describe but felt in my teeth. The crunch of metal on metal, a sound there are no words to describe it. It was the sound of hearts breaking and friends losing a military buddy, a coworker, a brother, a son, a father.

What my body prepared for and what happened left me disoriented for a moment. *What was that?* I expected a wreck, an impact, to be pushed, something more than a mere bump. It didn't match, something was off and it left me thinking I had imagined the light that has now disappeared again.

LEFT TURN, LIFE UNIMAGINED

We were in the ditch on the shoulder of the road staring out the windshield to overgrown pasture, replaying what had just happened. I had enough sense about me to pause. But then I saw him from my rearview mirror, and everything became clear that this was serious. A man was lying motionless an arm's length from his motorcycle in the middle of the road. If it hadn't been for the broken headlight dangling from wires creating a small patch of light next to him; I might not have seen him there.

A man just hit my car, or did I hit him?

"Oh my God, I just hit a man," the specifics were futile, nothing else mattered to me but the man in the road and his safety.

"Momma, what just happened?" Brooklynn sobbed. Hazel, who had been quiet the whole ride in the backseat did not understand what had happened. She knew she was scared, she knew this was not normal, she wanted out of her car seat. Her arms flailing with all her might begging for my comfort.

I don't know what to do, I thought.

An unexplainable calm fell on me like a warm blanket. This gentle peace allowed me to breathe, I grew still and suddenly I was overcome with the courage to go to him.

"Yes baby, someone hit us. Stay in the car and pray. Mommy has to go help him. Look at me, I need you to be brave. I want you to stay with Hazel and just pray."

"No, don't leave us..." and without a second thought, I abandoned them. Slammed the door on their pleas to stay and ran into the dark to a man injured on the road.

Please God don't let us both get run over in the middle of this road.

"Sir, are you ok? I am getting us some help!" I called out to him as I ran but no response.

The closer I got, the more I understood just how desperate a situation we were in.

"No no no, dear God no," I screamed as I approached and saw the bleeding from his head, mouth, and ears. Scared and shocked I fumbled to put in my passcode and instead tried to use 9-1-1, it denied my access. *"Crap, what's my passcode?"* In the darkness, hands shaking, muffled screams calling for Mommy coming from the girls. *Breathe, do it again,* unlock. I made the call subconsciously because everything going forward is distorted.

•••

I see this isolated moment in time trapped in a snow globe in my memory file. To this day it does not feel real. Completely consumed by fear and yet overcome with miraculous courage to face the unknown. Even when my heart was breaking. The Lord was with me the moment I called out for help. The single greatest gift he could give us, David and myself was his presence. I am eternally grateful his family would be able to say goodbye. Isaiah 41:10 says, "Don't fear, because I am with you; don't be afraid, for I am your God. I will strengthen you, I will surely help you; I will hold you with my righteous strong hand." If we learn anything from reading God's word, we will find ourselves in terrifying situations and we will need strength not our own. In time, reflection provides the peace to see and know it was God with us the whole time. He was there on the pavement when I had no light and when I didn't know what to do. He was with David and with his family as they processed their grief.

The hardest call.

"**911**, what is your emergency? Who am I speaking with? Where is your location?" The operator spat questions at me, and they stung like welts from a pellet gun.

"I don't know," I stumbled over words. My mind went blank. I didn't know my name at first. Not that I ignored her questions, this was now autopilot talking.

"Where is your location?" she asked me again with some urgency.

"I hit a man on a motorcycle, please help us," blurted out of my mouth. "I don't know the street name. I don't know where I am, " panic threw that blanket of peace to the ditch.

"I show you are located at the intersection of Estates Street and Davidson Road, is that right?"

"Yes, please help us!"

The operator began to walk me through the next steps, that blanket found its way back draped over my shoulders.

"Is he breathing?" the dispatcher questioned. I knelt down as close as I could get without laying my head on his chest. For a moment I thought he moved as if to say something but instead, he let out a long slow exhale.

"Yes, he is, but it's shallow. Sir, can you hear me? Stay with me, please. Can you hear me? Sir, help is coming, stay with me" I pleaded with him. *Oh, dear God, please! Help us!*

"He isn't responding," I told the dispatcher, and the tears were on the edge just waiting to be let out.

I did as I was told - mechanical. I do not know when, or how long, or even the direction from where the help came but suddenly there was a man; he stepped in and began chest compressions. He took over.

Another man appeared. I think he wore a gray beret, he is a faceless man in a wool hat. I handed him my phone so that the operator could continue giving instructions. I was shutting down, not voluntarily but I couldn't hear her. Everything grew quieter-muffled, and whooshing in my ears and the jumbled chatter. All I could do was pray. My spirit prayed, not with words as I didn't know what to say. I don't believe it was audible - my soul cried out. I knelt beside him holding his hand.

When state troopers arrived, minutes did not feel like minutes. It did not feel like a lot of time passed and it felt like forever had passed since that emergency call. I was in full shock, my jaw shivering uncontrollably. People were talking to me, but I did not understand them. My hearing went in and out. Every part of me shook with unnatural force. All I could do was hold his hand; my right hand held his. People swarmed us, it was chaos and yet in my small space of cement road next to him, everything was in slow motion.

I was on autopilot. I felt my conscious thought float above it all, fully experiencing an out-of-body moment. Observing. Praying. Floating above the commotion. Someone offered to help me; I felt their hands on my shoulders. "Thank you, but please go help my girls," I motioned towards the car. Brooklynn got out of the front seat. Her scream, "Momma, momma!" is something I won't easily forget. Hearing my daughter's voice sucked me back into my body and back to reality.

"Get back in the car baby don't come any closer."

It was too late. Not that the confines of the car were going to protect her from what was happening but entering the space made everything that much harder. She didn't get back in the car. Instead, she froze at what she saw. My innocent baby sank down next to the back wheel of my Ford in the damp dark ditch. Yet, I could not leave him to help her. The natural motherly instincts to rescue and shield her from the tragedy unfolding was overridden by the need to stay by his side. Next to my victim, hold his hand, and pray.

Responders cut his shirt exposing a military-type tattoo. I gasped that destroying his shirt might upset him later.

"Ma'am, you have to let go." the paramedic commanded me. "Clear." A jolt surged through his body and we held our breath, he responded.

This is when chunks of time are hazy. I can give an account of what I think I remember; I cannot accurately attest to the timelines. What is real, what was a perception, what my mind protected me from, or what was filled in the blank spaces? It is impossible to sort it all out. I imagine the power behind the helicopter that briefly landed to get him, but I don't remember.

He was safe now; he was going to make it. God was going to heal him. I was sure of this! I was willing to bet my life on my audacious faith. God was going to work a miracle, and I believed.

I had hoped or in denial or a mixture of both.

People stood around inside this intense bubble where the scene of the accident took place until it burst. Paramedics flew him away. I retreated to the nearest curb to sit down. I don't know if I was directed there or if it was the only thing that made sense. Strangers still had my children. I looked over at what appeared to be two women, whom I didn't recognize comforting them. Angels? One was holding Hazel and rocking her gently back and forth, her head rested on the woman's shoulder. The other woman had her arms wrapped around Brooklynn where I could not see her face. My daughters were held by strangers in my place. I watched them comfort my girls. I thanked God for their willingness to lend their mothering to my girls, but I could not will myself to move. To go and be that for them, their mother. I was paralyzed.

My phone made its way back to me and was in the pocket of my jacket. *Did someone bring it back?*

Love is, knowing.

For years we collected the Love Is cartoon strip. Keith and I would leave them for each other at random places like on the car dash, or on the bathroom mirror, taped to leftovers in the fridge or on a card. I loved when whatever little one-liner below the picture reminded me of us. Over time I think love becomes knowing, there is an unspoken language between soulmates.

Calling Keith's cell would have been a waste of time, he was lifting and wouldn't answer. My husband is a creature of habit, so I knew his cell would be sitting in a cubby in the locker room. I called the YMCA instead. I had programmed the number when the boys signed up for swimming. My legs couldn't muster the courage to go to my daughters, but I remembered that I had the number to the gym.

I asked the desk clerk to find my husband. "He is in a navy-blue Oak Branch Fireman Dept. cut-off shirt lifting weights near the front rack. He'll probably be on the left when you are facing the big mirror, his name is Keith Anderson." Without question she set the phone down on the counter as I could hear echoes of voices as I waited.

"Hello?" he answered out of breath.

"Honey, I need you!" Maybe there is a certain sound in your voice that gets straight to the point. You just know that you know something is serious and he knew because he did not bother with details. Maybe he asked if we were ok and I said no, but neither of us can remember.

In moments he was there, seeing him wade through the crowd gave me the courage to leave the curb and cross the two-lane road to where the girls were. I could now cry. If I had before now, I didn't notice but seeing Keith, the tear-gate opened, and I sobbed in his arms.

"I didn't see him!" I cried out. "I didn't see him!"

"Is this the husband?" an officer asked. They gave us some space.

He took the girls. I didn't talk to them, I doubt I even made eye contact. They were whisked away from the scene. I returned to my curb and sat alone just two feet from where he laid, patiently waiting while the troopers conducted their investigation. People began to collect, bystanders accessing, frustrated residents trying to get to their homes were forced to park their cars in the ditch and walk. The police had the whole area on both lanes blocked off. They watched me, glaring my way as they passed, I heard their whispers. I felt the piercing of their judgment. Talking about me as if I wasn't sitting within a few feet from them.

"Did she look both ways?" Someone asked another, gawking at this tragic scene. I answered in my head, "yes, I think I did."

"She said she did but can't remember if she looked left again before pulling out," they replied.

I felt their sorting of facts and snowballing assumptions as I rocked back and forth on that curb. I didn't know what to do with myself. I didn't understand what happened. I didn't even have the capacity to ask questions. I just sat in silence, watching, and being watched.

Goosebumps covered my body, I was numb from the waist down, my legs and feet were tingling and asleep. Hands fidgeting in my pockets, observing the business of officers with orange spray paint that marked out details of directions and splattered blood. Circles and arrows, a hidden language. It took the troopers twice walking around my car with a huge spotlight that had to be manhandled by two men to find the evidence of impact. I turned away; I could not even look at that car.

Sitting there I had nothing but to just sit in "it." This void of understanding what just happened. The shock of it all. I felt oddly empty. I replayed some things trying to understand what went wrong. *I stopped, I looked, I looked again, there were no lights...*

Over an hour went by and I called my mom but there was no answer. I called my dad and again no answer. Feeling desperate for a friendly voice I called my little sister Cammy who happened to be visiting them. It is the kind of call you never dream of making no matter your age. A call I have never in all of my twenty years of safe driving had to make a call like this as it was my first car accident. I don't get a prize for that fact. No matter what, this one accident is what will matter anyway.

"Hey, Jen what are you up to?" My younger sister was pleasantly surprised by my mid-week call. Her voice was so happy to hear from me.

I think my silence to her question alerted her radar. "Are you okay," her tone changed immediately.

"No, I'm not. Where's Mom? I was in an accident," my spirit was defeated. I'm certain she didn't recognize my tone.

"Just please pray for him," I hung up the phone, stretched my jacket over my knees, and rocked.

•••

How do you tell someone you hit a person? That you may have killed someone? Things the normal person would never consider, ever. I don't know what I said. I just know I was already broken inside. Confused, and lonely, incredibly lonely. My mom would have come at that very moment, but I told her the morning would be fine.

The following message was to my Vice-principal, a motorcycle enthusiast, and also to the math department lead, "I have been in an accident, I hit a motorcyclist, please pray. I don't know if he will make it. I won't be in class tomorrow."

My hand buzzed, and I glanced at their responses but could not process a reply.

LEFT TURN, LIFE UNIMAGINED

"We'll take care of your classes, Jenna." "We'll be praying, Jenna, don't worry about a thing."

My words felt assaultive. How did they digest that text? How do you even expect someone to respond? They were with their own families having an ordinary evening, and BAM, you receive a message that someone you know may have just killed someone.

My neck began to tighten, and the veins at my temples throbbed and pulsed and pounded. I was on my curb, the least of anyone's concerns, put to the side. I understand; I appeared to be fine, but what was happening emotionally and mentally was anything but fine. An EMT walked by, so I waived. In a hushed voice as if I didn't want to disturb, "could I please have some pain relief for my headache?"

"I can't give you anything unless you want to go to the hospital, ma'am," he replied.

"No," I whispered, shaking my head. So again, I retreated to the curb. I watched the officers walk around, measure distances, and mark the road with more orange spray paint. Circling, notes on clipboards, flashlights, and brief huddled discussions like analyzing a crime scene. *It was a crime scene.* I just sat and stared helplessly in shock.

•••

All scripture is a treasure, some verses stick to the surface of your heart a little better. John 10:10 "The thief comes only to steal, and kill and destroy..." I knew this verse by memory, but it got lost in translation from the heart to head for a time. My mind somehow made me the enemy, then made God the enemy all the while forgetting who our shared enemy is, Satan. Do you know with your whole heart why you believe what you do? During this time, I would wrestle with my faith. It is healthy to challenge your understanding. Some people call this deconstruction which is both celebrated and frowned upon. I questioned everything I ever knew and believed about myself, my character, my purpose, and who was God. I sought him in new ways and waited for answers. During this season I felt like I was on an island, just me and my thoughts, questions, and prayers. I could not look to the world or "man" for comfort. I sought only the Lord and that time as hard as it was, I now see as a gift.

Complicated case.

There are no protocols for people like me, so I waited while the people in charge deliberated what to do with me. I lost track of time sitting on my curb. There wasn't anywhere to go. I didn't know how I would face my girls anyway. The only place I wanted to be was at a hospital praying by the bedside of the man I didn't know.

The Trooper in charge invited me into his car to get out of the cold. He had some questions. I didn't know what to expect. Did he mean to sit in the back? He motioned to the passenger side.

Stepping inside a police car is intimidating. This one was spotless. I noticed the strong Armor All smell first and that there was zero clutter, not a speck of dust. I wondered if he was ex-Marine or type A or how he must have grimaced while inspecting my car. What he thought about my empty cups and straw wrappers, various papers from folders, and probably remnants of fast food in plain sight of the floorboard. He was busy typing away at a laptop station jetting out of the dash. I was terrified to bump into it. He turned down the dispatcher radio.

I watched him with my hands folded in my lap, my ankles crossed as he diligently filled out his paperwork. The only sounds were of his typing and the occasional pause to scribble something on a small notepad. That and the obnoxious sound of my breathing. The nervous silence was painful. My thumbs fidgeted for a few minutes and then I was soon picking my fingernails. I tried to concentrate on breathing quieter. I thought to myself, *am I always a noisy breather?* I tried to sit and accept the quiet. But instead, my mouth took over, and chit-chat erupted.

The suspect or perpetrator (in this case, it's me, I am the perpetrator) normally doesn't try to hold a conversation with their, "officer in charge." That is how he was introduced to me, "officer in charge." I didn't know how to play the role of perpetrator. *Was there a set of rules?*

"My second cousin is a state trooper in Paris, Texas," I blurted out. Then I quickly regretted saying that because family connections are not going to help me now. What if he gets the wrong idea?

"No kidding, what is his name? I am from Paris." The trooper said.

What are the odds of that? "Do you know Carter Moree?" He shook his head no, didn't know him. So I offered off a couple other Moree's and distant cousins but still he shook his head. I sat quietly and he continued working.

"My mom graduated from Paris High...go Wildcats!" I fluttered my fingers and smiled in his direction. Assuredly one of the most awkward remarks of my life. *This is not the time or place for jazz hands.*

However, this big cruel world got smaller, discovering we shared a "hometown." A connection between two strangers in an uncomfortable exchange after an unimaginable situation. The part of my brain that controlled inner dialogue had a brief break.

Paris, Texas, is a small town near the Red River. Paris was my childhood home away from home. Generations of my family still live there, a whole Moree clan from Honey Grove to Paris. This country town is where Keith and I were married. I chose it because I was baptized in that church after an Easter Sunday as a teenager. I knelt at the altar and was sprinkled with holy water in a blue polka dot dress with a shiny white belt. I had to remove my white straw hat. I remember how proud my Great Aunt Christine was that I had made this decision. The pastor's heavy hands-on top of my head as he blessed me smushed my blonde curls.

Every holiday we visited that church, and I got lost in a sermon a time or two daydreaming about the day I would marry here.

LEFT TURN, LIFE UNIMAGINED

It was also fun to say, we were married in Paris, Paris Texas that is. There is a fairly big rodeo that attracts cowboys yearly and an Eiffel tower topped with a cowboy hat but other than that it consists of an old town square, a few stoplights, and a Dairy Queen.

"You know the First United Methodist Church there right off the square, that's where my husband and I were married."

"The big one?" I nodded. "You're kidding? I know that church." He started to tell me something about FUMC by the look on his face, but he stopped.

"Today is my 3rd anniversary," he said a few seconds later. In that discovery I wanted to apologize that he wasn't at home celebrating with his bride but instead sitting with me.

"Happy Anniversary," I said. When he didn't respond I willed myself to silence. Stop. Talking. *Just stop, Jenna let the man work.*

Everyone knows of this church because it is huge for the population of the town, a focal point just off the square. FUMC of Paris is more than a century-old church known for the original stained glass, massive stone pillars, and a working organ where wooden pipes stretch from stage to ceiling. But the most impressive feature is it's topped with a copper dome and cross. This is the church that nurtured my love for Jesus. In my opinion, its architecture steals the show from the square's Italian marble fountain. When I think of Paris, I think of my grandmothers and my Great Aunt. I think of every holiday spent there and weekend summer getaways and the corner store where candy was 25 cents. But I always think of that church that symbolizes the blossoming curiosity of childlike faith in a man named Jesus.

The fact that I now sit in a State Trooper's car in the hot seat with an officer who shares a love for the same small town made this moment bearable in the strangest way. It wouldn't help me by any means with my case, but this was a tether cord of comfort from my past entering into an unknown new normal.

"My Great Aunt used to live in the little yellow house right off Main Street."

He paused from his work to again acknowledge what a small world. His expression lit up; he knew exactly what house I was talking about. I thought I caught a smile, but he continued to look down at his paperwork.

"Do you have these kinds of accidents often? A car with a motorcyclist?"

"This is my second one this week," he said solemnly. *It was only Tuesday, I thought.*

I would not have blamed him for asking me to remain silent. He was kind enough to oblige me with conversation. He carried on scratching his papers as I rambled.

The small talk made it feel more human. It was obvious I was nervous; he also knew the reality that lives would change or have already changed rather. The motorcyclist's and mine, but he refrained from informing me about all the things I would soon be forced to become accustomed to. A whole unknown world after accidents like this. Lawyers and insurance. Lawsuits and charges. Fears and mental disorders. Grief and guilt. It would have been too much to take in all at once.

I asked him about the other car and motorcycle accident from this week, "did they make it, the motorcyclist?" He shook his head with a sigh and a somber, "No, they did not." He had to let the family know as he would soon also inform the family of the man I hit. He would have to share a message that never gets easier: their dad was en route to a nearby hospital. While none of this conversation made sense, I mustered up the courage to ask him what I really wanted to know. What I sat there thinking about in the back of my mind the last two hours.

"What will happen to me?" possibly a selfish question in hindsight but a reasonable one.

He adjusted his posture, paused, and gave me a straightforward answer which I appreciated. His response was both diplomatic and professional in a police-ish way. Still, he was sensitive to the complexity of the emotions I was experiencing at the same time.

"I may be writing you a ticket for failure to yield the right of way, but I am not going to do that tonight." I nodded in acceptance. I felt that was minuscule and somehow unfair. I deserved bigger than a ticket, but I wasn't giving thought to jail time at this point either. I wanted to tell him that I did yield. I yielded to the best of my ability, I just did not see him. Thankfully I resisted the impulse to clarify.

He continued in his southern good 'ol boy accent, "If he makes it, you will be hearing from your insurance, and he will probably get legal representation. If he doesn't make it, then you will hear from me more, but your case will be reviewed. I or another officer will conduct a full investigation for the District Attorney and a Grand Jury will decide whether to indict or not." I nodded my head as if agreeing that made sense.

"Yes sir."

Indict, the word lingered in the air. A word I have heard before but used for other people, criminals, not in my normal vernacular. Certainly not directed toward me. Just didn't seem real, he was speaking about my possible indictment. As in arrested and charged.

"His family will more than likely seek legal representation and be in touch with your insurance." This nice man who should have been with his wife celebrating polietly spared me the details of the mess I was in. Life-altering trauma had just transpired, and I wanted to converse like we were just new friends chilling in a cop car.

What I wanted was for him to give me all the answers to what would happen now. During this conversation, he alluded that when he deals with these calls it isn't often good for the "other driver," most of the time he is arresting the "other driver." I am the "other driver." Cases like mine are "complicated." The truth is I was unintentional or not, a perpetrator, a part of a criminal investigation and I would never be the same. A few hours ago, I was a school teacher and law-abiding, safe driving citizen. A caring wife and mom. Just like that, the identity of who I was, was gone.

"Did you want to drive home? I can follow you in my car," he said once he was done with the information needed for a crash report.

"I'll get that report out to you as soon as I can." I nodded as if I understood. I could not even imagine driving now, the thought of getting in that car made me physically ill. I no longer trust my driving ability.

"No, no thank you," I stuttered, "my pastor and his wife will come when you release me." At some point, I received a text letting me know they would come whenever I needed them.

"Go ahead and let them know I am about done for now, so they can head here."

I sent out a quick text, "Almost done, can you come now?" They were waiting at our house with Keith and the kids just down the road.

There comes a time when the brain has had enough. You take mental notes but you check out and say nothing, this was that point. I watched him in silence as my need to know "things" was tapped out. The things that I was trying to process made the car smaller. Officer Kurt carefully opened a soft brown leather satchel with a brass latch. I could tell it was well-loved. Worn around the edges and the strap looked soft but not ragged. He pulled out a wallet, his wallet. I saw his driver's license picture flash a very different person from what I just witnessed. Seeing the man smiling made my nose and eyes sting, blurring my vision. A tear trickled down which I wiped away quickly.

I hope I can remember him that way, with a slight smile. I wasn't sure how to act, was it ok for me to be looking toward the officer? Do I look out the window and stare at the darkness of someone's property? Was it disrespectful to look? Invasion of privacy? I was too afraid to ask any questions.

Wait, where are his glasses? Did someone get them from the road? I panicked silently. Do I alert Officer Kurt he had glasses?

He continued to fill out information scratching away on papers. I sat in silence, alone with my scrambled thoughts. This too would become a new normal, withdrawn inside, alone with my relentless thoughts.

Going home suddenly felt terrifying. How will I face my girls?

•••

Time after time during the most horrible circumstance there would be this little glimmer of how God was in the details. I don't believe in coincidences. 1 Corinthians 14:33 "For God is not a God of disorder but peace, as in all the meetings of God's holy people." It's like when our older daughter was needing brain surgery and we fell into the hands of one of the most experienced surgeons in North America. She also had a complicated case, and in the end, doctors would use words like "remarkable" and "textbook" to describe her diagnosis, surgery, and recovery. Of all the Troopers working that night, finding one that had the slightest common ground gave me peace. The fact that my former work colleague and soon-to-be counselor would be working that night was ordained. God's promises guide our path and that includes the people he brings into our lives. It all has a purpose.

Every little detail.

A brick-red truck glided past us, startling me at first when it parked between the Trooper's car and my own. Why would someone come so close to us? Who were they? But then I realized my friends were here to get me, and relief washed over me. I was so preoccupied with the health of the man I hadn't noticed when they had opened the road back up to traffic.

One of the things that did not disappoint about our move to Lake Hills was stumbling upon our church family which led to an amazing community group. We did life together, and somewhere between sporting events, bible study, dinners, and prayer requests, they have become an extension of our family. After Hazel's surgery, they rallied around us, going above and beyond. But this should win a Nobel prize for friendship; when they are willing to pick you up from the side of the road near midnight from a State Trooper's patrol car without hesitation.

Last year Pastor Philip was in a similar accident. A man threw himself in front of his truck purposely (a different truck). The man did not survive. We watched him grieve and as a community, we stood beside him as he healed and processed his role in such a tragic end to life. Who would ever suspect that his testimony would later minister to me in such an intimate way? He knew in some ways the struggles I would face.

Philip's wife Sharon is an instant friend to all she meets, a servant-leader and a mama-hen. I'll never forget her pulling up to our house as we were still unloading boxes from our move. Her boys were my husband's new offensive line. My cheeks were red from a heatwave that hit early June. She pulled right up, greeted me with the sweetest smile and started unloading a feast. Sharon was the first smiling face to welcome us to our new school with a hot-out-of-the-oven homemade lasagna with all the trimmings.

LEFT TURN, LIFE UNIMAGINED

Cheesy buttery breadsticks, a Ceasar salad, and a layered chocolate pudding dessert. In case we didn't have them handy, and we didn't she included utensils and folded napkins. She brought disposable cups and a gallon of sweet tea. This woman was a saint, I didn't have to cook for two days.

Sharon is the first to initiate prayer with even the slightest hint of worry in your voice and an all-in attitude when you need help. Sharon is an avid hugger so once I was given the signal that it was all clear to exit Officer Kurt's car, I practically fell in her open arms on the side of Estates Road. Nothing needed to be said. I just cried. I felt my hair gently slip through her fingers as she comforted me. Like a little girl I buried my head in her shoulder and she comforted me. I love Sharon for that hug. It was the hug of all hugs and exactly what I needed. I let out as much of the pent-up sobs as I could, preparing to face my family, face my girls. She helped me to the truck, gave me her hand to hop in and she, not me, carefully buckled me in.

She had the heated seats on so I would feel cozy, the Christian radio turned down to a hush, but the faint melody was a familiar worship song. She offered me a throw for my lap. Every detail was thoughtful. She took care of me as if I were fragile, and I was. Philip drove my car and we quietly followed. Later, I would learn they counseled Keith on how to take care of me over the next few days. Make sure she is eating, watch for anything unusual in behavior. They warned him I may have trouble sleeping, cry unexpectedly, seem different, or distant.

It was nearly midnight when we arrived at our humble townhome. It didn't feel the same, coming home. There was no relief that I was now safe in my own space, out of the cold, and reunited with my family. I couldn't help but think that I am here, and he is in the ICU. Or worse what if he didn't make it. The big kids were awake, Hazel had fallen asleep in her sister's arms. I was in what I would describe as a trance. *Philip and Sharon stayed around for a few minutes but as hard as I have tried to go back to this place, I have no real memory of what was said.*

"Can we sleep in the girl's room tonight, Mom?" Connor asked. I heard them but didn't answer, or maybe I said, "sure," in my head, so Keith gave the okay. The boys instinctively knew to take care of their sisters, but they didn't know how. A quiet pain had swept through our home, and everyone felt its ache. How else does a big brother protect his little sisters? But to stand guard and watch over them as they sleep? The boys made camp on the floor of the girl's room. I would normally assist in the making of pallets, but tonight I couldn't participate. I just floated about, not speaking. There was no energy for words, let alone spreading of sheets, layering of quilts, and tossing of pillows.

I wanted to lay down, but a heap of clean towels covered the bed. I glanced at the floor, and I could have easily collapsed. I started folding them. It was midnight and yet I was oddly lining up corners and smoothing over edges before wrapping them in perfectly stackable tri-fold squares. I placed the rather tall stack on the nightstand where they slowly began to tilt, losing their precise form and the top two toppled to the floor. I didn't flinch or huff or sigh or curse that the freshly folded towels landed on the floor. When Keith came to bed, I was a motionless ball, my knees tucked up to my chest still in my clothes from the gym, my pillow soaked with tears.

"Honey, don't you want to change?" Keith's voice was unusually tender. He isn't known for a hushed voice or gentle anything. He is tough, protective, assertive, but for the people he loves, gets to experience this side.

Blood on me had not registered, even quite possibly on my hands. I hadn't washed them, and I was most certainly around blood. The many orange circles were proof. *His blood is on my hands, I thought.* A shower made sense, but I had to force myself to move. Keith sweetly helped me to the bathroom, "Do you want a bath or a shower?" "A shower," I whispered. He adjusted the shower and I immediately sat down, bringing my knees to my chest. He gathered the things I needed but could not do for myself. He brought me a towel from the stack, something to sleep in, and God love him, a cup of hot chamomile tea. I tried to categorize what I was feeling with what I have experienced before and I had nothing, no familiarity. It wasn't a new mom kind of exhaustion, or the first week back to school tired, not fighting the flu kind of ache, or the emotional exhaustion from watching your child recover from surgery but something unexplainable. This feeling was dark and weighted. It was tangible like a presence was there looming in the bathroom watching my breakdown.

I feel like I have just fought for my life. What kind of self-absorbed person am I? It was him, the man in the road, the one I hit, he was fighting for his life, not me. Tears just streamed; every ounce of my being poured out in weeping. The closest I ever felt this low I found myself staring into the toilet when I lost a baby at eleven weeks on the 4th of July 2011.

My heart refused to accept it until I touched the blood and tissue, seeing it on my hands made it real. "No, no no, this can't be happening!" "Why, Lord?" I began to shake uncontrollably. I let out a wail as tears flowed. It's my fault, "I take it back I want this baby, Lord!" *How can I just flush? Should I bury this baby?* I gave into the brokenness, head rested against the porcelain when a calm settled down over me like a mist. I didn't want the kids to find me in this state, so I locked the bathroom door. On the bathroom rug I cried out to the Lord to receive my baby that I already loved. I miscarried, and my heart shattered. The moment I stopped praying I was bombarded with accusing thoughts. I blamed myself. I questioned my sin, was this a form of punishment?

Did I not take care of myself? Did I do too much today? Have I not repented of something from my past? Was it because at first I was not thrilled that I was pregnant? How will I explain it to the kids? This will crush them, they were so excited. Lord, I don't understand! I turned on the shower and sank curling my legs up to my chest and let the water wash away my tears, washed my wounded body and cleaned the remnant of a baby already so loved that was not meant to be. With a splotchy face, I looked myself over in the mirror, put on my red, white, and blue tie-dye "Happy 4th" shirt, and emerged from the bathroom prepared to pretend my way through this celebration. I joined the family in the van, looked at the three little faces that were bursting with anticipation of the night's fireworks. "What's wrong babe is your stomach upset?" I leaned over to whisper in Keith's ear before leaving the driveway, "Honey, we just lost the baby."

•••

When I crawled back in bed, I was ready to lay my head on Keith's chest and hear the rhythm of his heartbeat. The reality of death was so close I needed to be reminded of life.

A voice in my head began to scold me. Why did you not see him? Did you look? Did you look again? How did you not see him, Jenna? This voice knew me. How will you live with yourself if he doesn't make it? *I don't think I can, I replied back.*

How will I explain it to the kids? What will happen to me? Oh God, I don't understand!

The thump-thump, thump-thump of his strong and steady heart soothed me for a moment, something we did when we were first in love. Always trying to sync our breathing by listening to each other's heartbeat. Knowing I needed a distraction I reached for my phone and opened to social media.

"What are you doing, you should rest?" Keith questioned my decision to get on my phone.

"I want to see if I can find him, the officer gave me his information."

I searched his name, and he helped me. Two profiles in our area with his name.

"I think I found him," Keith said. When he turned his phone towards me, I immediately recognized him. There he was standing with pride by his motorcycle, a picture similar to his driver's license. In a shirt like the one from tonight. I was relieved to see him. I felt like praying over his picture and imagined my hand stretched over his hospital bed. But then my heart stopped when I read father to three in his bio. I don't know what it feels like to be shot but I can imagine this was close, the news ripped a hole in my heart. The need for a miracle grew three-fold. I began to writhe in pain of guilt with the realization that I didn't just hurt him, but them.

Lord, please heal him. Have mercy Lord, touch his whole-body Lord. Please let his children see a miracle. I pray you to make him whole Lord. Be with the doctors and nurses and give them wisdom and insight into what he needs. Please let him live fully restored to health. Oh God thank you no one else was hurt. I am so sorry for this; I don't know what is wrong with me or how this happened but please make it right. Heal him, Lord, please. From his head to his feet, all of him. Work a miracle, Lord. You have the power to heal him. I ask this in Jesus' name. Amen

I laid there so still Keith thought I had fallen asleep but really, I was just lying there praying, afraid to fall asleep.

"Good night honey, I love you," he whispered. "Forever and always."

"Forever and always," I replied. My thoughts returned to praying, *Jesus, please heal him*! "Please Lord, let him make it!" I said out loud. Keith thought I was mumbling in my sleep. *I'll do anything, let him make it, heal him, please! Work a miracle, please God work a complete miracle.* I turned on the bible app and let it read to me the Psalms of David, hoping the narrator's voice would lull me to sleep. The scriptures that would normally comfort, began to sting. Scriptures poured over the wounds of my heart and with every thought of God allowing this, my heart broke. With every mention of David, a sting. For the first time in my life, I felt hurt by my faith that God had a purpose for my life.

∴

I described this time and the weeks to follow that I felt like my brain was stuck. My brain was a browser with too many tabs open. All its energy was devoted to why this happened. Faith is a muscle; we exercise it and the stronger and bolder our faith grows. Romans 12:12: "Be joyful in hope, patient in affliction, faithful in prayer." It is like this scripture was written backward on purpose. Because when you are patient during affliction and faithful in prayer the effect will be abundant joy. That first part of the scripture is nearly impossible and finding joy even harder during a crisis. When Jesus is our source of joy, hope found in his promises will always restore that joy in time. I truly learned the essence to pray without ceasing through my accident. Oh, how I wish it did not take a tragedy to bring me to the place of praying continuously. Jesus is the very reason I still breathe deserving of my every thought.

Facing the hill.

Daybreak hit differently; I was hungover from heartbreak. The sunrise did not bring a promise of a new day. I didn't know what news I would be waking up to. My first thought was, *Lord, heal him. Please heal him.*

I lost count of the times I woke from visions of the accident. Over and over, I was there at the stop sign waiting for him to come over that damn hill. Waiting for the headlight to emerge from behind the tree and pass by me. I saw the shadow of his bike and I waited alone in the car. My heart raced, that I would open my eyes into the dark of our room and stare at the shadows of the wall. They would transform to bike handles and pass across from the window to the closet door.

I could barely keep my eyes open but there was this fight to resist because of what I would see when I closed my eyes. Maybe it wasn't as horrific as I remember? Maybe God healed him through the night. Maybe he was awake and mad as hell at me for pulling out in front of him? *Just keep praying God hears your prayers. Keep the faith, Jenna.*

Deep inside I knew the outcome, I just had this feeling. The Holy Spirit was there to comfort my sorrow, but I denied it as the voice of the enemy. I must stay positive and speak-life. I must carry on, hold on to hope, take authority by the blood of Jesus.

The Lord was preparing my heart, I was just too stubborn to listen. *Hold on to hope, Jenna.* "Believe for the miracle that will come." "Don't think about these things Jenna, he will be okay, keep the faith." I would tell myself every Christian catchphrase I knew and anything other than a narrative of complete miraculous healing flashed in my head; I would rebuke that thought and call it evil.

My phone flashed a missed text from my mom, "Just leaving Dallas, will be there soon." I forgot she was coming; she would have dropped everything last night to be with me if I had asked. A mother knows her children and she knew in her gut that something wasn't right with me.

"No mom, don't come now, tomorrow would be better." Before I even made it downstairs to tell everyone, there was a knock at the door, and she was there.

Mom, now known as Nana, is a fierce mama bear when it comes to protecting the people she loves. When I was pregnant with Connor, her very first grandbaby, she parted the crowds in front of me that summer of '02 at the 4th of July fireworks display. Like a lineman lead blocking the most precious of things, her grandson, she cleared the way. Mom split the crowd with a stare and a motion, weaving us back to our car after the festivities. There were an estimated hundred-thousand people there that night. I was kept in a protective bubble, no accidental bumps into my growing belly.

The pain she must feel, the anguish that this was out of her control. She couldn't protect me from what was to come. I made a mistake and there are consequences for mistakes. A very helpless feeling for a mother at any age, watching her child struggle through heartbreak. It hurts to imagine the pain I put her through. Surely, she felt the absence of her daughter's hope-filled spirit. I was there physically but I wasn't the same. It broke my heart that I could not hide my pain for her sake.

I wanted to ask her to take me there, "the scene" but before I had the courage to ask her, she brought it up. "Let's go by where it happened," she suggested softly. We both wanted to see it. The stop sign, the hill, the oak tree, the orange spray paint on the ground. I needed to see it in the daylight. I hoped maybe something would make sense, that the light would have the answers to why and how this horrible accident could have happened.

Getting into my mom's passenger seat I felt frail. I didn't know how I would feel riding in a car. I clutched the door for security. Driving was now a place of fear. I directed my mom a few turns and there we were driving the same hill he did the last few moments before the accident.

God, give me the strength to face this hill.

I started to tremble as we approached the turn for the hill. Her blinker became incredibly loud as it ticked. I became more curious than afraid, more connected to this place that was now sacred ground. Fear did not overtake me as I anticipated but instead, I abruptly felt nothing. Completely numb. Some kind of psychological wall suddenly appeared.

Returning to the scene didn't help, if anything I felt more confused. The oak tree's leaves were beautiful. This was a massive tree, at least 100 years old. The morning dew on the grass was peaceful and this patch of country was not an evil place. The shadows were gone, no blind spots or obstructions blocking my vision. If he had only seen the 100 yards of pasture, he might have veered around me.

Mom thought the entrance to Hidden Lakes was too close to that hill. "It's dangerous," she insisted. The hill was the reason this happened! We always want something tangible to blame, it's easier to blame a person in this scenario. Blaming fate or "these things just happen" are terrifying words because it subjects us all to the unpredictable nature of life. Or worse, to blame God and my heart began to shout, "No, blame me, not God!"

Cars would just appear over the hill like a mirage breaking up the beauty of the countryside. What stood out like a sore thumb was the bright orange spray paint. The hidden story of the markings headed to the north entrance of the lake. They could have easily been mistaken for road work. But I knew what the arrow meant. The X was in place of his bike, the small circles were a piece of him, they highlighted the awful truth. I had a sea of thoughts from visiting the scene 12 hours later but two that stuck out as odd.

The first absurdity was I wanted to touch the bloodstained road. Part of me wanted to curl up where I knew he had laid to be closer to him. Just stay there awhile and plead forgiveness. I wanted to be the person on the road instead of him. I fantasized about doing it, laying down. I imagined abandoning all common sense and giving in to the temptation. What it would feel like without any reserve for the deadly consequences.

Ridiculous, I fought myself! Are you out of your mind? Scolding the voice that would urge such a thing.

The second impulse was an overwhelming desire for rain. When I say wished for rain, I don't have the vocabulary for a stronger word. I begged for a horrendous and torrential downpour of rain to wash away the memory so boldly outlined with neon paint. The wish for it to be erased became so strong I would have fallen to my knees and scrubbed the road until my hands bled right then.

We left with no peace; we drove in silence to the next task. I stared out the window swimming in thoughts. I felt my mother's struggle to speak or to just let me be. She resisted the need to know what I was thinking. As painful as the silence was for her, she respected my need to just be still.

Next on the agenda was the driver's license office, my address was notably not correct on my license as observed by Officer Kurt.

"I assume this Fort Worth address is incorrect?" He asked me while adjusting his posture straight up, squaring his shoulders against the back of his patrol car.

"Yes, sir, I just haven't got around to changing it." I then gave him the correct one. It's a wonder I could recall my correct address as I felt my brain was mush.

"You should take care of that," he suggested.

"Yes sir, I will do that right away." An oversight on the to-do list when we moved but now, I wanted to cross every t and dot every i. Because when sorting all these legal things out I didn't want, of all things, my address to be wrong. Going into the building was strange. I had to compose myself. I wasn't concerned about a line; no, I was worried I would have to tell someone about the accident. To make things worse I could not just change the address as intended.

"Are you a donor?" the clerk asked. Now more than ever I want to be a donor.

"Yes ma'am," I nodded.

"Ma'am you will need to take another picture," she said in a stereotypical DMV fashion.

"Wait I have to; can I just opt for the one currently on there?" My plea was desperate. I had already waited for 30 minutes, wondering if anyone in the room knew the man on the motorcycle. From the moment we walked in I wondered; did anyone know him? Fidgeting with my black cardigan as if adjusting it would make things feel more comfortable. The truth was, I didn't feel good in my own skin. *Did anyone recognize me from last night sitting on the curb?* Taking a new driver's license picture is always annoying. I would rather do anything else in the whole world than take this picture at this moment. Regretting not giving half a care about what I looked like before we left! It's not hard to imagine what a person would look like the day after the worst night of their lives. My hair was unbrushed pulled back tight in a greasy ponytail. I faced the camera, but I couldn't face my reflection this morning before leaving. *Would I look different?* It would be 10 to 14 business days before I would get this little keepsake. I stood on the white line, she said, "smile." I tried to comply. I would always know that picture was taken the day after my accident. The worst day of my life is documented.

⋯

Looking at that hill and it very well could have been the tallest mountain. Climbing it felt like judgment day and the old oak tree, my Calvary. Psalm 121:1 "I lift my eyes to the mountains— where does my help come from?" I was beginning my journey to walk out of the initial shock and seek full dependence on the Lord. He would be the only way, when he says he is the way, the truth, and the light, he meant it. This was bigger than anything I could face on my own. Strength to face each new day burdened beyond words, all God's grace, and to face my family. Strength to face that hill, the camera at the DMV. When I look back it was a miracle. God's word is true. We can't imagine walking the roads that are not ours because his strength pours out as we need it and when we need it.

It doesn't look good.

All of my family were gentle, and people walked carefully around me. It was strange the absence of arguments over what was playing on the TV, who was in charge of the remote, or who had more mac and cheese in their bowl. When it was time for Mom to leave, my stomach sank. Looking into her pained eyes I made sure I thanked her, really thanked her, and I told her, " I love you, Mom." As she drove off, I thought for the first time what if she doesn't make it home? What if that was the last goodbye? *Will I deserve that? I felt like maybe I did.* I carried on sitting, being still, and silently praying. This is the essence of prayer without ceasing. *Supernatural healing Lord please work a miracle. I would repeat that thought, Lord please, please work a miracle!* I was fine until about 8:07 pm and my eyes became fixated on the time. *Was this when it happened? Or was it closer to 8:10?* My heartbeat became rapid just trying to decide and suddenly I had to push my shoulders back to give my lungs more room to breathe. This was anxiety, a new feeling like I was desperate for air. My brain was working so hard to understand that the automatic responses like breathing took effort. *Why don't I know the time? How insensitive, I should know this.*

"Have you heard how he is doing?" my mom casually asked before she left.

"The officer said he would update me, maybe he has the night shift again," I answered. The phone buzzed not much after 8:30, the call I both wanted and feared.

"Hello Jenna, this is Officer Kurt..." He let me know things did not look good, he had more heart trouble on the way to the hospital. He reminded me that it was best for me to not try and contact the family. I think I asked to come and give my respects or at least alluded to something of that effect. His call left me with a pit in my stomach. Hope faded. I hung up and felt nauseous. All life drained from my being, and my limbs felt weak. I retreated upstairs.

Notifications flashed on my cell, three message requests from people not on my friend's list. I opened the first one and it said. Do you know what you did? He has three kids... I stopped reading and deleted the other messages without opening them. Good sense would have told me to close out the app, but I needed to know. Secretly, I had been watching the updates on a local Facebook group. The group's purpose is to update our small community about breaking news such as weather, arrests, some town gossip, free stuff, lost pets, and car accidents that are blocking traffic. I watched the comments about the accident that shut down the road over by Hidden Lake Estates. I lingered on every post. The man was in the ICU and didn't look good. Consumed by the comments I physically stopped breathing, my eyes stung and then spilled over with tears when I read a woman's post. She had picked up his children. "I've got Dave's kids; we are on the way to the hospital. Please send all the prayers their way. It doesn't look good."

They probably don't want my prayers, but I am praying anyway.

I imagined them holding each other, comforting one another, assuring each other it will all be okay. But then I saw the comments that began to pop up, little bursts of anger and other explicit emotions just as fast as my internet refreshed more and more comments concerning the accident out on Hidden Lake would appear. It had caught the attention of the town like wildfire spreading. They had no idea I was among them, that acquaintance they knew.

"People need to watch where they are going."

"Probably on their phone." another comment.

-Reply, "Or drunk."

"People are in such a damn hurry and need to be more careful, no one is safe."

"I hope this city does something about it."
"She deserves to be in jail!"
-Reply, "They didn't arrest her?"
-Reply, "Who do I need to call? This b!—- should be off the streets!"
"How many people have we lost to stupid drivers?"
"Heard she ran the stop sign and didn't look."
Reply, "Who was she, what was her name?"
"She will just get a slap on the hand and get away with murder."
Reply, "Did he die?"
Reply, "No, listed as critical."
"She will rot in hell for what she has done, his poor family."
"I can't believe the selfish drivers in this town. I hope they take her license, so we are all safer."
"His poor kids, how awful someone should tell her she wrecked a family!"

Fifty-two comments deep and nearly one-hundred likes, dislikes, tears of sadness and angry emojis and counting. My shame on public display. I stopped reading, as each one grew more aggressive to the person who "ran" the stop sign.

It was me; they didn't know yet, only a matter of time, but it was me.

"I stopped, I know I stopped, I looked, I know I looked, I always look!" My guilt and grief kept me from defending myself on that post. It would only make things worse, and I did not feel worthy. Besides, what could I say to satisfy their anger and grief? The comments did not frustrate or anger me. I believed them all to be true and I thought much worse of myself and my actions. What apology could I give that would even make it better? None. There isn't any explanation in the world that would help even if I had one. Nothing was good enough to explain what happened.

I didn't understand what happened, he came out of nowhere, but then that sounded like I blamed him for what happened. That was the furthest from the truth. I blamed myself, the only one responsible. *Let them sling hate at me, I deserve it*, I thought. Better to blame me than God. The weight of causing someone to turn from the Lord was more than I could bear. I wanted to close myself off from the world. Life would never be the same. I didn't sleep and I didn't eat, and all my energy was devoted to prayers for the man I hurt. The family I hurt. The community I hurt.

Dear God, please let him live! Please spare him. I will do anything, take me, maybe it should be me. Please God work a miracle. Cover him in supernatural healing! Please Lord, please let him live. You can do this; I know you can. I have loved you my whole life, served you as long as I can remember, and I know you can heal him. You healed Brooklynn; you can do this Lord! You heal people every day, please him too. Be with his children, I'm so sad for them. I hate this. Hate that this happened. Oh God let them have a moment, fill them with peace. Give them a sign, comfort. Please, please, please hear me, Lord.

My abdomen began to cramp, and I folded over to pain, completely overwhelmed with all the emotions. My body had waved the white flag in defeat, and I began to bleed unnaturally. I lay there in anguish and confusion and in my own filth. The tears just streamed from a well deep within, my eyes raw from weeping they burned and stung. Tears like creeks after a heavy rain have cut and carved the terrain, it hurts to cry. I never knew it was physically possible to weep like this.

⋯

The sweet presence of the Lord in times of sorrow is sacred. You only know if you know. Psalm 34:18 "The Lord is near to the brokenhearted and saves the crushed in spirit." My whole being was crushed for the family who lost David. I could not imagine forgiving someone like myself and therefore I remained in complete agony. If we cannot forgive something, how could we then accept the forgiveness for ourselves? It is impossible because it is connected. Of all the many lessons my accident taught me, that of forgiveness was woven into all of them and it was the hardest and last step towards healing.

Unanswered prayers.

Life just kept moving on even though I felt it shouldn't. I needed life to pause so I could catch up. The sun graced my window, as it would on every other day, yet this felt out of place. There was no smile to acknowledge how beautiful it was. I grew bitter that it was a new day.

I noticed the dust on the blinds. I couldn't enjoy the beauty of daybreak. Before I would normally admire and thank God for crystal clear blue skies, birds migrating and sunshine but instead I was surprised I made it another day. Like I was the one laying in the ICU bed. How dare I acknowledge the day as a blessing? People are hurting. I don't know what I expected, maybe to not wake up, or wake from this nightmare. I couldn't imagine living this sad life forever. I won't be able to do it.

I rallied the energy to roll out of bed to teach a class that starts in 15 minutes. "The kids need me to show up," I thought. They are the delight of my day and the only time I feel normal. The joy of teaching has been my only constant and sometimes my only reason to face the day. I have not disappointed them like everyone else around me. "Thank God I don't have to go into a classroom." Suddenly that thought triggered an angry monster, *was this why God opened the door to teach from home? You knew this would happen, God? Are you serious God, of course, you did, but why?* My heart was in two camps, grateful to not have to face students in person and irritated that God knew this was the only way I could continue to do what I love, which was teaching.

•••

It was a scary and exciting decision to leave the brick-and-mortar school for this new unknown and intimidating online learning platform. No one had heard of it, teaching from the comfort of home but public education. The goal was to be home, maybe keep up with laundry, write a book, or go back and finish my master's degree. I was so surprised to get the email about the open 8th-grade math position. I love teaching math and I would not give up my middle schoolers for anything. The thing about math is that there are several ways to solve a problem, it's reliable because there is always a solution. And when a student has that ah-ha moment and you witness their confidence grow, it's the best feeling in the world! When I was little, I would force my younger sister to sit down with our stuffed animals and a chalkboard to play school. I was, of course, the teacher. I am certain she was the only first grader to learn her multiplication tables.

We were on the verge of transition with my husband's school. We had heard horror stories of how coaches can be pushed out, but we had never experienced the cutthroat politics of a small Christian school until now. I knew working virtually with the flexibility to move would maybe come in handy, I was right. We are accustomed to moving schools but never leaving on bad terms.

I married a personal banker with a safe, secure office job. We soon felt called to ministry. Ministry led to volunteer coaching and one opportunity led to another. For the last 13 years, he has been coaching all sports that he can get his hands on in small private schools ever since. Right before Hazel's surgery, I could sense tensions. "Christian" organizations are still composed of imperfect humans, it can get messy. The Bible is full of messy people, none of us are immune. God prunes branches, a nice way of saying he moves people and here we were living it. I remember saying maybe God gave me this job because he knew Keith's position would be changing. It was a reasonable theory.

The turmoil of contract changes had something to do with it I am sure, but the accident, the accident was no surprise to God. That realization filled me with rage. A God of love could not be so cruel. I could not imagine facing a classroom full of bright-eyed children ready to learn pre-algebra in person. How could I face them wondering if they saw me differently, or worse knew him. What if one of his daughters would have been my student? I would not have made it, but online I could fake a smile in my voice for the kids that knew nothing about what I had done. For a few minutes, my mind focused on something I love, encouraging young people to believe in themselves.

My classroom was a sanctuary, a place where every problem has a solution and students thought I was fun with my math jingles. My classroom was my escape from it all. I forgot briefly that there was a man I hurt fighting for his life. Only once did a student ask me, "Mrs. Anderson, are you sad today?" His question exposed my mask, so I ended the class. Buried my face in my hands and cried, the tears dripped to my keypad.

This was also the day of my nervous breakdown. My pastor's wife Sharon had called to check in on me right after 4th period and warned me not to read the paper. So naturally, when we hung up, I googled it. The local newspaper published little snips covering the recent accidents in town but mine was front and center and the most detailed. *Jenna Anderson, 36 years old of Lake Hills, TX driving a black 2015 Ford Explorer... Local Teacher runs a stop sign and causes a major accident. Local Veteran critically injured. Motorcyclist Care Flight to Ft. Worth hospital listed as critical. The investigation is ongoing. Charges are pending investigation.*

Before I even finished reading, I lost all control of my body. Once again, my knees buckled as I began to shake. First, my lower jaw and it spread to my hands. I hit the floor and laid my head against my desk chair. Nausea set in and my agony almost took me out. Breathing was strained, I was heaving, starved for air.

◆◆◆

Leaked information, by who? Why? Why would people of our town need to know how old I was, what I was driving, where we lived? Would they be waiting for me outside? Would they hurt my children to get revenge? I was inundated with more worry, fear, sadness, shame, that even my thoughts began to stutter. I couldn't even process a cohesive thought.

My anxiety grabbed fear's hand and ran wild in my imagination of what could happen. Mrs. Anderson ran the stop sign. That's a LIE! I screamed at the article. There was something significant about seeing it in print, I started shouting at my laptop and just melted to the patch of carpet under my desk and screamed and punched the floor with the back of my fist. "I st-st-stopped at that sign; I know I stopped!" "I looked and di-didn't see him!" Shouting into the air, shaking my fists in frustration.

"I looked; I kn-know I looked!"

When I came back to reality, I called the county chaplain, an old friend. Dr. Knox was, "Glad I called." He said he had heard my name over the dispatch the night of the accident. He was not allowed to make contact unless I requested it. I wish I had known that. Did someone explain that, and I missed it? Not that it would have changed anything but would have been nice for someone to pray with, to sit with on that curb. He said he would call the station and talk with the chief, somehow/someone had disclosed information prematurely. He was disappointed. I was distraught.

My crash report is still not yet typed up and the investigation is still, "ongoing."

"How can they do this?" I cried out in desperation. He agreed it was a little unusual for the paper to release so many details about a car accident. At this point, there was not a fatality.

"Come by the church office and check-in with how you are doing, stop by anytime."

We hung up and I kept repeating the words, "I stopped, I know I stopped, I looked, I know I looked. I did, I know I did."

❖❖❖

JEN EIKENHORST

I don't know how long I laid there on the floor. I don't remember picking myself up either. Lots of blur during that time but what I do remember, I value. God's word says his eyes are on the sparrow, he knows the numbers of hairs on my head and his provision demonstrates that this is literal and not figurative. After my daughter's brain surgery which took 6 hours, I was called back to a recovery room. The nurses took me to the wrong child, let's say I nearly lost my mind in that children's hospital. However, I caught a glimpse of a small foot peeking through a blanket 20 feet away and I recognized it. Was it the Holy Spirit? Was it a miracle? Or was it the instinct of a mother that knew the very form of her tiny toddler foot?

If I could spot her, then our loving God knows us more than we can imagine and cares for us more than we will ever know. Psalm 40:12-13 "For troubles without number surround me; my sins have overtaken me, and I cannot see. They are more than the hairs of my head, and my heart fails within me. Be pleased to save me, Lord; come quickly, Lord, to help me." In the confusion of the hospital mix up or on the floor processing the newspaper article, it was the Lord that helped me through both.

Am I a killer?

There was a knock at the door just after dinner and it was Officer Kurt. "Good evening, I don't want to disturb your dinner, but I wanted to come by in person and let you know the family is preparing to take him off life support. They are getting a few things in order because he is a donor." I thanked him for being so thoughtful. When the door closed, the air was squeezed out of my chest and along with it was my hope.

I began to cry uncontrollably, my stuttering returned. My behavior didn't make sense to me or to my loved ones witnessing me break down over and over. Crushed in spirit I completely blanked out. I wanted to go to his side, to tell him sorry one more time in person. I had a vision of him in a hospital bed, his children surrounding him. These were their precious last moments with their father. I would not be welcome there. As much as that closure would possibly help me, their peace meant more. I never wanted to cause them any more pain than I already had. My quota of hurting anyone, ever, was all used up for the rest of my life here on earth.

Dear God, please hear me, there is still time. Please let him not be in pain. I pray for supernatural peace for his children and family. Send them comfort that only you can give. I lift them up to you. Please God, they need your presence of comfort to surround them. God why, it's not supposed to be this way. Holy Spirit, please do something. If he can't be fully himself take him home peacefully, but only if that is your will. I beg you for a miracle. I am so sorry David. Oh God, David I am so sorry for this. I hate this Lord; how can this be real? Why? I don't understand how this happened, make it right Lord.

My prayers were not answered, and I felt betrayed and abandoned by God who I believed worked miracles.

A post on social media had an update to David's condition, it read, "David is now at peace. Please pray for his children during this difficult time." I read it again. And a third time, it didn't feel real. I needed to lie down.

The only solace I could cling to is that his children had time to say goodbye. To be given some time. He was a donor, through that selfless act his legacy lives on. What an honorable decision we can each make. His passing was what I should have prepared for, but I hoped for the miracle of healing. Hope died when it became a reality, how could God redeem this?

Did I not pray hard enough, because I haven't stopped praying! Was I not specific enough to supernaturally heal him? I am confused right now God, he was there, right there! I thought he would be okay. Was there a mistake, he wasn't really gone? He was right next to his bike, we weren't going fast, he looked like he would make it. His glasses didn't even break! So many people are saved every day from crazy horrific accidents, and he was right next to his freaking bike, why? I am so mad God. Why is he gone? Why Lord, why did you not heal him? Was it his time? Then why me, how could you let me hurt him? Is this punishment for something? I don't get it. Maybe you aren't good, maybe everything is a lie. Have you abandoned me, God? I don't feel you! Why can't I feel you, I feel so lost and so alone.

With his passing, I labeled myself a killer, the world would now see me as an accidental killer, and David's family would see me as a murderer. David was gone, I hurt many people and there was nothing I could do to make it better.

My heart crushed under the weight of the news. Time felt like an enemy once he was gone, now we waited for what would be decided legally from the District Attorney. The words from Officer Kurt came flooding back, "if he doesn't make it, we will be in contact about the next steps." This was the strangest feeling. Waiting on whether I needed to turn myself in, it just didn't seem possible. *Wasn't it just a couple of weeks ago I boasted of a squeaky-clean driving record?* My first accident is now possibly vehicular manslaughter or negligent homicide or any other combination of legal terms and charges. Regardless of what would happen to me, the most pressing concerns on my mind now were, how are his children? Are they okay? Do they hate me? If I were in their shoes, I would hate the person who did this.

In it, together.

The kids have now set up camp in our room, none of us were sleeping well. The six of us are in one room. All four children slept on thrown-together pallets at the foot of our bed stretched from wall to wall, lumps of blankets and pillows and stuffed animals. Reminders that we are in this together. Maybe that's where they felt they could be close to their mother, maybe they wanted to protect me, keep watch. They had no idea how they held me accountable. All we could do was survive the day and dread the night.

I lay awake and cried as I listened to their sleep noises. Someone would be inhaling and another exhaling, there would be murmuring and snoring that resembled a bear from the love of my life. It was comforting to have this nightly orchestra. Maybe this is a gift, five reminders of why I am still breathing. *Oh God, I love them so much! I don't deserve them, they know I need them!* The quiet of the night was the hardest. Just after 2 a.m. Brooklynn woke from a nightmare, sat straight up to vomit all over herself. This is the second time she has done this.

"I had a bad dream," she cried. Everyone worked to clean her up and switch out her blankets. We worked quietly not to wake Hazel. Normally, I take the lead on things like this. It was a "mom-thing", but Keith and the boys swooped in and handled the mess while I followed Brooklynn to the bathroom. On autopilot I turned the shower nozzle to warm and placed the soiled pajamas in the sink. When the water was perfect, I motioned her to climb in, she sat and pulled her knees to her chest in one motion. I balanced on the edge of the tub to wash her hair half asleep. Grabbing the no-tear shampoo and lathered a generous portion. Rinsed with Hazel's hair cup. We said nothing as this was now a seamless routine, gently pulling the pieces of undigested food out of her hair. Wash, rinse, repeat. She cried, I cried.

LEFT TURN, LIFE UNIMAGINED

"I'm so sorry momma," she said into her knobby little knees.

"Shh, Sissy it's okay. You did nothing wrong." *I thought to myself, it's me that's sorry baby. It's my fault for your nightmares.*

Dear God, what does she see when she sleeps, please take this from her? I caused this, please heal her. She should not carry these thoughts, give them to me God. Give them to me, not my baby! Lord, she loves you deeply, please deliver her from these dreams. Give her peace, have mercy on us Lord. I believe you have destined her to do great things. She is hurting right now, and I can't take it. Do this for me, for her, for our family. Let her have peaceful sleep, free her from the scenes of the accident. Thank you, Jesus, thank you, God. Amen.

Just as the amen left my lips my thoughts drifted to darker places. I entertained the bashing from foreign voices and called it mom-guilt.

Time just kept passing, 72 hours is an unimaginably long time in the wake of trauma, every minute ticks and every hour drags on. The days are the hardest. It's all so hard. So much has happened, and it was only Friday. Of all the weeks, my school had the first field trip of the year planned to the Natural Science Museum in downtown Fort Worth. The day was overcast and gray. We walked through the fog to the entrance of the museum; the cool mist blanketed the area. We were greeted at the bottom of the stone steps by my principal, she paused from ushering parents and students to wrap me in a mama-bear hug. It is a rare find to have both exceptional leadership qualities and a depth of compassion that breaks down industrial walls. Mrs. Troy is gifted with both. She was surprised to see me but glad I was there. If I needed more time off I could have taken it. I didn't know what was right. Being at home I would feel just as horrible as I do now try to resume normal life.

"Have you had any updates?" she asked. Her voice full of hope. And I braced my soul to speak out loud words that hurt to say.

"He passed late last night. He was a donor." She didn't need any details and when I had trouble looking her in the eyes, she swooped me in with another generous hug.

Keith and the kids came with me to the museum. Not just to drive but also to care for me. They were all so tender and attentive. They didn't let me out of their sight. All of my family hoovered, ready to protect me, catch me, hold me steady, and remind me to carry on. We were all here walking marble halls and admiring art and exhibits. I didn't feel deserving, tears meandered down my cheeks, dripping from my nose. I looked around at paintings and sculptures but thinking of his family and their grief. Crying in public didn't bother me but wondering if I looked like a killer did bother me? Such a misplaced thought. What does a killer look like? I was wearing jeans and a long sleeve gray knit blouse. Did I fit the specs?

No one would suspect the real meaning behind my puffy eyes. My fellow teachers were all so caring, but it was awkward. Everyone was unsure how to comfort me. Should they ask, not ask, I could see their hesitation. They tried their best but there are no comforting words for someone who accidentally killed an innocent person. None.

Charges, trial, retainers, bond, these terms were all legalese I could not wrap my mind around. Time was ticking. I expected to hear from Officer Kurt soon, maybe no news was good news. That felt weird to think, should I follow up with him on how that was going? That also felt strange. Of course, I would comply wholeheartedly with the consequences of my actions. After all, he had the right of way, I made a mistake and there are consequences to mistakes.

Dear God, who can help me?

•••

Proverbs 3:5-6 "Trust in the Lord with all your heart and lean not on your own understanding; in all your ways submit to him, and he will make your paths straight." This verse was one of the first I memorized as a young girl. Proudly I stood at the front of a room near a small podium and recited it for my Sunday school teacher. As a reward, she fished out some candy from a glass bowl. It's been hidden in my heart ever since. I desperately wanted to be on the straight path, I didn't choose to leave it for the bumpy road I was traveling.

How did I get there, was this the plan? I honestly don't know and will not know until I reach heaven and ask Jesus in the flesh. But I am guessing when we get there the pain of this world won't matter and I won't need an answer. The path in this verse is not the one God intended, his plan was perfect but then people and free will and sin and choices and... The straight path is the one where he guides, it's his hand you hold through the terrain. Your grip gets tighter when you lose your balance, step in a pothole, or trip over a protruding root or fallen branch. He catches you and you know you are on the right path.

Love abounds.

The days are long, but the weeks fly by, that's how the saying goes. The person who coined that term has not experienced heartbreak like this. The hours drag on, and each passing day shocks me that time and life are still going. I find myself fixated on the day of the week. Counting down the minutes until the next Tuesday. How could a week go by? And how will another week pass that I'm still breathing?

Keith reminded me it was Sunday. "I have a surprise," he said. Plans were made with my parents and sister without my knowledge to meet in Fort Worth. I remember mom mentioning that Dad and my sister wanted to see me and the kids. But I had no recollection that anything was set. Except it was very much set. For the first time in fifteen years of marriage, I was cut out of the planning process. My normal duties of wife and mom would take a back seat. It just happened each passing moment I shrunk inside myself and became less recognizable to those who loved me. Despite my attempt to hide from life, it was dragging me along. It marched on at a different pace and I was having trouble keeping up. Somehow groceries were bought, the pantry full and the milk in the fridge was in date. The lunches and dinners were made but not by me. I didn't even notice that I had been released from these duties.

Fort Worth is a historically rich town and is a favorite pitstop on the drive east from where we live now to Dallas to visit my parents. Keith and I love an occasional getaway or date night in downtown Fort Worth. We have many treasured memories running around hand in hand amongst the lighted trees that adorn the streets. Sometimes we opted for a family adventure to the Japanese gardens to feed giant koi or skip down sunken water fountains. Sometimes our only intention was to discover eclectic food trucks and explore the city with no plans at all.

LEFT TURN, LIFE UNIMAGINED

As a child, my parents would take us here for festivals or the rodeo. They all knew I loved this city, and they planned this outing for me. To wake me up, bring me back, possibly a cure for my broken heart. I thought I was masking my feelings but maybe they knew I was slipping away. This was their attempt to remind me I am loved. Keep a flicker of hope burning in me until my heart could catch up to reality. It was a sneaky move pulling off this family outing and one I am grateful for.

We all arrived at the Stockyards District about the same time. I got out of the truck, and I was met by the arms of my daddy. He is a 6'2" man with peppered gray hair and he smells of Irish soap. He is my avid tennis player, Dad's club participating, tickle-monster hero. The first man I ever loved, the best Texas two-step partner in my opinion, and the parent patient enough to teach me to drive. What I admire most about my daddy is his intentionality to uphold integrity. Not that he is perfect, but he is quick to remedy mistakes and own his downfalls. Despite the fact that he has the opposite political and spiritual beliefs that I hold, we have never argued across the dinner table. We listen and appreciate each other's viewpoints. He and mom celebrate that they raised independent women that think for themselves.

The first thing he did out of the car, was scooped me into his arms. He hugged me with an embrace that broke down my wall of pretending to be okay. I used his shirt as a Kleenex. I had never felt a hug like this before. He kissed the top of my head and I felt like a little girl at that moment. Like the time I got lost in a department store, it was that kind of hug when I was found safe. I was released into that hold long enough to cherish it for the rest of my life. Even on my wedding day when he walked me down the aisle. With pride and tears in his eyes he kissed me before passing me to Keith; this kiss paled in comparison. This embrace was different, it was one of desperation to hold his baby. Like one of fear of losing her, and one of thankfulness that I was still there.

I was able to enjoy it long enough to have a memory before the voice reminded me that his children would never again feel this kind of love. His children were missing this, the love of a father to his daughter all because I failed. That same voice that snuck in and countered every sliver of happiness or normalcy was becoming more consistent. I could not quiet it, tame it, or tell it to go to hell. The voice was growing and becoming my narrative.

Outwardly, we appeared to be a normal family. Grandparents with their children and grandchildren doing the touristy things. In reality, we were a family with their lives upside down. Parents worried sick but trying to hide their fear of what might happen to their oldest daughter. I was worried about them worrying about me. I was also feeling the burden that I have ruined all of our lives. I was tormented every moment by my thoughts. My family could feel me slipping into a depression without knowing if I would have the strength to recover. But here we were strolling and smiling, walking, talking and soaking up the sights of the "old west," together. I've had at least a dozen thoughts that I am a killer, and a couple dozen more that reminded me of my shame.

Lunch was at a BBQ restaurant famous for peanut shells that dusted the floors and crunched under your steps. The crunching sound like dead grass reminded me of the ditch the night of the accident. Old Country music played in the background from a yellow and brown jukebox that entices you to hum the melody and mouth the words. "Oh, I've got friends in low places..." We all chimed in with our best Garth impersonation. This song took us back to a time when we had no idea what whiskey was or the blues we sang of. With that last line, "I'll be okay," the tears once again came flooding in and I felt ashamed I would ruin the day.

LEFT TURN, LIFE UNIMAGINED

The air smelled of hot sweet rolls and perfectly charred smoked meat. It stirred my hunger a little, which had not happened in almost a week. Hazel and her cousin were in heaven gathering piles of dirty peanut shells. "Look mommy, snow," she let handfuls flutter from her hands and drift to her feet. While waiting for food the kids rode a small merry-go-round, the adults made small talk. No one mentioned the accident. It was the elephant at the bar staring at me over my shoulder.

We feasted on brisket so tender it fell apart, so good you lost your manners and licked your fingers. Baskets were systematically refilled with golden buttery rolls that you could palm like a softball, perfect for soaking up meat juice. I washed it down with sweet tea and splurged on a piece of coconut pie nearly 6 inches tall topped with a pillow of meringue. The kids shared banana pudding and practically licked the bowl clean. These kinds of meals happen for birthday celebrations and not just because. It was a constant battle to reign in my thoughts to be fully present and enjoy them. But I did enjoy it, and I felt the sting of guilt for doing so.

"So, food," I announced with a satisfied smile, and everyone laughed. My parents looked puzzled. It's an inside joke meaning "so full." To relieve our full stomachs, we all walked over to watch the cattle drive. Crowds of locals and tourists enjoy this tradition. We line the cobblestone streets and wait for the cowboys and cattle to pass. I took it all in, the sounds of the hooves clanking on the stones, cheers, and cowboys whistling commands. Nothing like a whiff of manure to remind you you're alive.

The highlight for me besides the slice of perfect-meringue pie was riding a restored conductor train. It takes passengers from Fort Worth to Grapevine and back. Sitting inside was like walking back in time. I admired the woodwork, it's a lost art, rubbed my hands across the velvet seats which made it feel royal. Glancing from kid to kid, all were smiling. I wished I could go back in time. Why did we not do something like this before? Being together just because.

Looking out the window the world looked calm seeing the joy in my family was everything, every minute I treasured. I simply did not feel worthy to be so blessed to have this day.

No one noticed when my eyes would suddenly just fill with tears. I got good at wiping them away before they reached my cheek. I wore sunglasses that seemed to help, at least they didn't say anything.

I was entertaining the voices that taunted me with lies. Whose voice is in my head? The day trip was not just a family outing but an intervention.

"Jenna Lynn, you take care of yourself, you have people that love you." My mom was doing her best to control her own tears as we said goodbye. Dad and sister were just as emotional not knowing what would happen. I can only imagine the strength it took to make it to their car and break down once we were out of sight.

"I know you love me and I will, I mean I am, I will see a counselor tomorrow," I assured them with as much confidence as I could muster.

This incredible day was winding down, we headed back home and I watched the sky melt from orange to raspberry sorbet soup. I thought about what that sky might look like from David's view. Heaven sounds so nice right now.

The clock on the dashboard summoned me, 8:07 p.m. I would find my thoughts entangled with the events of the accident. I held my breath until a sufficient amount of time had passed. "By now he was in the care flight." "This is probably about the time Keith got there."

It made me nervous we were still on the road. The world would stop, and all my senses would bring me to a place inside of my memory. A chamber devoted to the cold air of October 4th, the jagged road pavement, the panic, the small headlight that dangled from a '97 model Harley. I don't know how to describe what I feel. If sadness and emptiness were fused and magnified, that would be how it felt. However, this day was one of the most memorable of my adult life. It was a constant tug-of-war between being grateful for a day like this and not deserving of a day like this. I put the sadness in a box and didn't speak for the rest of the night.

•••

I was walking a labyrinth of emotions. My transgressions could hinder the people I love, the people David loved, and I was taking on responsibilities that were not mine to bear. Psalm 69:6, "Lord, the Lord Almighty, may those who hope in you not be disgraced because of me; God of Israel, may those who seek you not be put to shame because of me." Our happiness is not contingent on other people, to make us happy or allowed to steal our joy.

Only the work of the Holy Spirit can mend some wounds. Whether you were the one who was hurt or the one who hurt someone else, we are the same and we are both at times. During this time of guided isolation, meaning I withdrew but was surrounded and protected by loved ones; I also had many memories brought to the forefront. Times when I was hurt and needed to forgive. Times when I hurt and asked for forgiveness. Times when I spoke out of line, held onto bitterness, or betrayed a friend with a slipped secret. All situations worked out and made me stronger and more humbled, the maze of memories left a trail of wisdom nuggets. I wasn't on the journey to reach the Goblin King but on a quest for God's peace. Acknowledging my faults was another layer of refinement.

Divine appointments.

I sat down on a well-loved loveseat nestled in the Lake Hills Church of Christ. A few years ago, I worked in the office down the hall as Dean of Students for the school that rented the church during the work-week. I wore a range of hats which included meeting regularly with church staff. I had not been back in this office since I resigned from the position to care for Hazel after her surgery.

These walls hold in confidence countless tales of the human condition; pain and loss, secrets and confessions, budget concerns, weeping, and wailing. Marriages have been fought for and dissolved on this couch. People seeking advice for wayward children and many first responders seek spiritual counsel here, as it is home for the county Chaplain. But people like me remain silent, the anguish of the accidental killer is a story seldom shared. I was only the second person who caused accidental death to come to him in his career.

I wrestled with myself to ask for help because I didn't feel I deserved it. I wasn't the one who lost a loved one, how dare I? It took every effort to breathe, the courage to face the day let alone getting dressed. Driving here was a small miracle.

Dr. Paul Knox and I had many conversations in this same office where I now sit. Often, we just waved when passing in the hall right outside the door. Nothing of this nature, usually we stuck to small talk, squaring away details of shared school and church space.

Dr. Knox is a gentle soul. He wore thin, black-framed glasses that slid down his nose when delivering a sermon or when chuckling at his own jokes. Which was frequent, he is always smiling and laughing, almost like a tick. It's enduring. He has a smile as big as Texas and an even bigger servant's heart. I could not think of a time when I did not see him with a smile, he wore it faithfully like his uniform. You will find him riding in a patrol car, assisting with difficult welfare calls, walking the hospital hallways, or volunteering with Lake Hills youth.

Now there was me, the other driver, not the victim or the victim's family but the perpetrator, the unintentional killer. I haven't come to terms with this situation. I didn't know how to be this person.

Last week I was a tired mom of four active kids, a supportive wife, an expert multi-tasker, and an ordinary school teacher. Last week I would have described myself as a prayer warrior, strong in the faith, and a good-hearted person. None of those descriptions fit anymore. Who am I now?

Why am I here?

The last time I sat in a counseling session was in 2001 for premarital counseling with my then fiancé, now husband of fifteen years. We were hopelessly madly in love, just bursting with hope for our future. Could not stand to be apart. The pastor met with us over the three months leading to our wedding day. We talked about children and chores around the house. We talked about who would pay bills and what to do with disagreements. Nothing ever prepared us for unplanned pregnancies and premature labor and long-term bed rest. We didn't talk about lost jobs or switching careers or genetic disorders with chronic medical conditions or the heartbreak of miscarriage. I feel like the scenarios we toyed with did not scratch the surface of what life would throw at us. We have lived through the unimaginable in a decade and a half.

Marriage vows are not for the faint of heart, all jokes aside, that tough line about "for better or worse," that was, for now, we were living the worst. We could have never dreamed up this living hell. Without question, therapy was long overdue. I should have had my rear end parked on a couch like this time and time again. I never allowed myself the time. At this moment, I had no choice but to relinquish pride or whatever it was that kept me from addressing my mental state. My psyche was crumbling with each new realization of this life-long burden. My heart was already shattered, this was an attempt to save my sanity.

I was living in mental limbo. There were so many uncertainties about our future. I could not imagine happiness again or joy without guilt. Losing hope day by day, a lonely state for sure.

Sadness had stolen my voice, so I thought this meeting would be a waste. I imagined I would sit there and just cry for an hour or so. He, being the caring professional would tell me how to feel like myself again.

I believe Dr. Knox is a gifted listener. His simple hello was the magic word to unlock all the emotions. He handed me a box of Kleenex and I used about half of them. During this episode, I ended up on my knees on the floor. Not even sure how I got from here to there, but I let it all go. It was freeing, an out-of-body experience. I left myself and released gut-wrenching groans, sorrow spilling out from my soul where it had been festering for days. I was talking to Dr. Knox but hashing it out with God on the floor of his office. I finally admitted what I had felt all along, forsaken. Abandoned by God.

"Why did this happen?"

"Dear God, why did you let me hurt someone?"

"Why did I not see him? Is there something wrong with me?"

"His glasses didn't even break; they were just lying there beside him as if he took them off."

"Why did God not answer my prayer for his healing? Why?"

I reenacted the scene, I crouched down over a pillow on the floor, and I felt as if I was back on that cold road. My knees felt the pressed imprint of rock pavement. I was no longer here, but there.

"He looked like he would be fine, we did all the things they told us to do. I held his hand; did he know I held his hand? I protected him, Dr. Knox. I abandoned my girls for him, they were so scared, and I just left them alone with strangers."

LEFT TURN, LIFE UNIMAGINED

This is the threshing floor of grief, but I didn't know I was grieving. I cried until there were no sounds left, just rocking, and wincing. A face that only the deepest pain can produce. There were moments of abrupt pause. I would catch my breath. Blink out tears to look over to my trusted confidant searching his eyes for all the answers to my endless questions. I begged him to tell me everything would be okay. He couldn't do that because there were no certainties. Dr. Knox sat resolutely still holding space, the anchor to a shipwreck of emotion.

"I feel like a monster," I shouted!

"I hate myself as much as I hate what happened."

"What will happen to me, Dr. Knox?"

"Have I ruined everyone's lives? Their lives and our lives?"

"What if I go to prison? Can a marriage sustain that?"

"Was this the purpose of my life, to hurt someone?"

"Jenna, breathe. Inhale deep cleansing breath, in through your nose. Now exhale slowly," he said gently. I'm sure I was near hyperventilating and making him nervous.

"I love the Lord, Paul, I do. I do" I looked at him, "Did I do something, and this is my punishment?"

"I love you, Lord! "I cried out. "Do you hear me?"

"I love you, Lord!"

"I've loved you for as long as I remember!"

I said it aloud over and over. Maybe 20 times I declared my love for the Lord. Sometimes I said it as a plea, I said it as a groan, I said it as if I was trying to convince myself that I still had my faith. When I paused it wasn't just to catch my breath but waiting for God to answer back that he loved me too. I needed to hear him, "Precious Jenna, you accepted my son Jesus as your savior long ago and I love you still, I am here with you."

Dear God, I have served you my whole life. I don't understand! I have told people of your goodness, your faithfulness. I feel like a liar! I love you Lord so how can this have happened? Jesus, I need you to pray for me! I don't know what else to say.

When the flow of words and groans began to slow, and my temples throbbed. I quieted my spirit; I had exhausted it all. He witnessed the meltdown of a woman he once knew to pray before meetings and hand out detentions for tardy teenagers. How different these two women were. He did give me a few directives. "Stay off social media, or any media," he said with a fatherly tone. He suggested I hire legal representation. The other was to try and write letters to David or journal or go for walks.

"How did I get here Paul? I don't know who to call?"

"If I were ever in trouble I would call Frank Strawn, he's the former D.A. in town. He is a little blunt, but don't let that scare you. He is tough, to the point, and good at what he does. Exactly the person you need in your corner. Oh, and just to warn you he has a patch over his eye. His demeanor can be somewhat rough, but he is solid, and I know he can help you. He is the best criminal defense attorney in our area."

"Paul, I need a criminal defense attorney?"

"I have talked a little with the guys down at the station, this should all be just a formality. You followed the law to the best of your ability, and this was a terrible accident."

I nodded but it didn't feel like this was, "just an accident."

"But Paul, it could happen."

"Yes, there is always that possibility. Right now, let's take this one step at a time. Call Frank."

Anything Paul would have suggested, I would have done. I was so lost, thankfully I had trusted people surrounding me.

"Jenna, I'd like to check in with you weekly, you check in as often as you need to, here is my number. Let Keith know I am here for him too." He was committed to my healing and the other county chaplain would attend to the victim's family. *Victim. You have a victim, Jenna.* I heard his name echo in my thoughts, bouncing around like thunder, his name beat against my insides. He was all I could think about, him and his children.

I left the little Church of Christ office feeling some relief. This was just the first layer. We scheduled an appointment for the girls. Dr. Knox had a friend that specializes in trauma with children and play therapy.

Lord, I love you, but my heart and my mind are at war. The battle between what I feel and what I know to be real. My soul feels torn. I lost everything when I pulled into that lane. He lost everything.

"Look at all that you have," I felt the Lord say. Do you mean my family, Lord? *Yes, I am grateful for them, without their support I wouldn't have the will to go on.* "Let me be your strength." Lord, you'll have to be my strength because I've got nothing. This is bigger than me. "Yes." What about his kids, will they be okay? "Let me take care of his children," said a voice in my spirit.

•••

I had heard of the threshing floor used in sermons from time to time. I experienced it first when we did not yet have a diagnosis for Katy aka "Brooklynn" after months of headaches and seeing specialists. A member of our church had reported me to CPS for leaving our youngest son (7 months old at the time) in the car while I dropped off groceries for the Thanksgiving feast. It was drizzling rain and darn if he didn't fall asleep as soon as I drove up to the church. That was a shameful experience, and it was in the midst of the time we were fervently seeking answers to my three-year-old's headaches. I hit the floor of a church office and wept.

I was suffering as a young mom, questioning God and if I was good and how much more could we take...sound familiar? This is what he does. Job 39:12, "Will you have faith in him that he will return your grain, and gather it from your threshing floor?" Refinement is a painful process, it's where we find our truth. Here is

JEN EIKENHORST

what I know about the truth so far, I am a sinner saved by the grace of God and I will need to fully depend on him, every day until he calls me home.

Facing the mirror.

When we moved from our quiet suburb cul-de-sac in Fort Worth in exchange for 601 Dixie Dr. #300 Lake Hills, Texas, there was no burning bush that we were on the right track. This quaint townhome that has been home for over a year now never felt homey. Two years ago, when we were notified that our small private school would be closing for good, both of us were out of a job, we panicked. We made decisions in haste, which led us to accept the first door that opened. Maybe we had not prayed enough over if this was a door or a distraction. Selling our house was impulsive in hindsight. We were just "winging it" by moving for a coaching job and believing everything would eventually just fall into place. Sometimes a leap of faith is a lack of wisdom, either way, it's what we did. The path we chose, we made together and with the best intentions. I believe that, whether it was a path or a detour, we love God, and he works out all things according to his will.

Still, it was a risk, everything was on the line to leave the metroplex and plant roots in a smaller town with fewer options for schools. But we had a strong faith in God as our provider and faith in each other to pull through. The little money we made selling our little 1980 sq. ft. home on Comiskey Way to an investor paid off some debt and afforded Chris to surprise me with my engagement ring. We had sold it at some point to help make ends meet prior to the current financial crisis. He always said he would buy it back. I was in the garage sorting boxes and packing when he nearly leaped from the car to get my attention with his beaming grin. Spun me around to face him so fast I nearly lost my balance.

"Babe, what in the world?" I was so caught off guard by his behavior.

"Give me your hand." Without hesitation, he had grabbed my left hand and slipped on the three-stone white gold ring just as he had done fourteen years ago. "It's not your exact ring, but it's the closest to the original I could find. He choked up on saying these words, "I promised to get it back." I looked up at his glistening eyes, he meant those words and he always keeps his promises. A little over a year later we would be navigating much more treacherous waters than pawning an engagement ring.

Lake Hills was a chance for a slower pace of life than the metroplex. Less traffic, a place where it would feel like family. We downsized a few hundred square feet to save money. Every home side-by-side has a different fun tropical color. Smaller yards with less maintenance, we aren't responsible for things when they break.

Before the accident, many of my prayers were dedicated to contentment and meekness, both admirable qualities and struggles for me personally. Always dreaming of more was a problem.

The more I dreamed, the more I was forced to be joyful in my circumstances. I remember reading Matthew Chapter 5 and thinking meekness was something I lacked. God was working on my heart to release some strongholds so I would pray to be humble. I asked God to make me meek. Be careful what you pray.

For days since the accident, I have avoided my reflection including the mirror above the sink. But because I was gracing the world with my presence, it felt necessary. A week has passed, seven days since it happened and five days since David met Jesus. It's shocking my heart has not given out. It was time to put my big girl panties on and face myself, "I look awful."

It's been a week and I've aged ten years. Your skin can give away your testimony. Wonder what someone will see when they take time to look at me? I haven't felt like this since the first time I looked in the mirror after losing my virginity to a boy who manipulated his way into my heart my junior year of high school. On a hot July evening one month before turning 18 and beginning of my senior year, the moon saw everything. It all happened so fast. I felt like a liar, I had vowed to save myself for marriage as a gift to my future husband. *Sorry, God, I broke my promise to you.* I'm a bad Christian I thought, so much shame for what I had let happen. *I wonder if I look different? Will people know I've lost my innocence? Will people treat me differently?* I slipped into a season where I didn't recognize myself then too, but that is a story for another time.

I'm fine, I lied.

*D*o *I look like a killer? I wonder if I look different? Will people treat me differently? What would make me not feel like this?* I can't numb this pain away. Even if I could, I don't deserve any less burden. His family will always feel the sting of his absence. Why should I have anything less?

"Honey, what are you wanting to do?" Keith called out. He thought I was talking to him and not mumbling like a crazy person to myself in the mirror.

He was sitting on the edge of our bed waiting for me to come back and explain what I wanted. I imagine he was unsure how to support me through my erratic behavior. My sudden jump out of bed to get into real clothes startled him. I'd barely moved or spoken in a week.

"I just want to buy a little something. Have a little memorial, maybe some flowers, and some balloons, that's all." I smoothed back my unbrushed hair into a bun. Doing my best to avoid his blue eyes. This simple request to answer him left me flustered.

"How much money are you going to spend? We don't have money for this right now and the insurance already sent flowers and a card."

"I'm sure that freaking covers it Keith, flowers and a sympathy card," raising my voice and shaking my head.

The frustration was not from what I wanted to do but because of how tight our budget was. With less than $50 to our name, his concerns were valid. My desire to do a little something in remembrance left me torn. But my mind was made up. What difference is $20 going to make when you are this broke?

It felt like the right thing to do. The last thing I wanted was to fight but I felt so strongly, I was ready for one. Explaining my needs took more emotional capacity than I had. I was the smallest porcelain teapot under crazy amounts of pressure. Tiny cracks were beginning to form. He must have picked up on how difficult this was for me and so he backed off. Avoiding what would have been our first argument and him breaking open what we weren't capable of putting back together yet, my heart.

"I just need to do this, okay? I don't know why but I need to do it."

I grabbed my glasses and purse so he too stood up assuming he would need to drive. He was standing between me and my fear of the outside world.

"No, babe, I need to do this alone." How my words must have made him feel? The worry I caused. Honestly, I wasn't well, and he could see through my facade. This man knows me better than anyone. When my mind is made up, there isn't much that will change it.

"Are you going to drive? Are you sure about this, Jenna?" He used my name. His concern tempted me to get defensive, but I resisted the urge to snap back. The truth is I didn't have confidence in myself, so I needed him to believe in me, even if he faked it.

Nodding my head, I shut down all emotion, locked it away. I was a brick wall. I made my way down the stairs darting straight for the door when four faces who had overheard the conversation met me with surprise. I took a deep breath and put on a confident smile.

"I'll be right back, I promise. It's just down the road everything will be fine." Thinking about what I said made me feel like a liar. The accident was also just "down the road," and they knew it. I looked into the eyes of my children and lied. "

I'll be fine" I assured them with a smile.

Was I really fine? Define fine, it's subjective. The grocery store where I was headed was right behind the YMCA, where I was that night. I'm sure he thought that he was fine too. Death is a swift teacher. The longer I waited to drive, the harder it would be to find the guts to get behind the wheel.

"I love you," I called out and waved. The kids all protested my decision with whimpers. Keith was now standing ready to hug them, comfort them and wait with them for my return. The decision to leave was made in haste not knowing how I would feel.

∴

It was not in my own power to get back behind the wheel, and to this day, I face my trauma each time I drive. The triggers are relentless, and anxiety could easily overtake me, but I keep fighting. Sometimes in life, we do things despite fear. We leap and expect God's divine power to show up and sustain us. The saying that God will never give you more than you can handle has been weaponized in our culture. Acute trauma like sudden death and the collapse of the world as you know it is more than any one person can carry alone. We must depend on the supernatural strength of the Lord; He gets all the glory. 2 Corinthians 12:9, "But he said to me, "My grace is sufficient for you, for my power is made perfect in weakness." Therefore, I will boast all the more gladly about my weaknesses, so that Christ's power may rest on me."

A memorial for David

My body and spirit walked out to the driveway almost as if I was normal, like the me before. From the house to the driver's seat without thinking. Once I was in, it was a different feeling, it felt like closing a coffin. Closing the door made a suction sound I never noticed before. I began to shrink, gobbled up by the challenge of sitting in the car that hurt him.

There was a stale smell, and I felt unusually cold. This car has sat parked since being driven back from the scene by Pastor Philip. My feet didn't reach the pedals. The seat pushed back to its max, the steering wheel a little high. Trying to make adjustments to fit me felt like too much effort. It felt wrong, dirty. *This car killed David, what am I doing in here?*

Sitting alone in the car used to be a moment of solitude as a young mom. I sat with myself, listening to my inner dialogue contemplating the decision to drive. What was I thinking? I gripped the wheel, my heart racing and paralyzed with fear. *You can do this, you are fine, it's fine, do this for David. Nothing is going to happen.*

My thumb and forefinger began to press harder against the key, and I felt my heart begin to twist and thump harder than ever. Jumping in a way that was not natural for hearts to feel. My fingers began to shake.

Something flipped a switch because the anger monster rallied above the sadness. Powerless, I couldn't do it. Frustrated tears erupted. I wanted to cuss and put my fist through the wheel. There was a growing list of things the accident had stolen and adding driving to the list felt defeating. "What the hell am I supposed to do not drive for the rest of my life?"

I started to go back inside and ask for Keith to drive but paused when I passed his truck. I don't hate the truck, maybe it wasn't me but being in that damn car.

It was worth a try. I'm short, driving the truck is awkward. I have a makeshift booster seat with my old '98 yearbook that I keep stashed under the seat for the occasion I do drive it. The theme that year was, make your mark with a giant thumbprint made of all the senior's names. "I really hate that clever pun right now!"

I drove past the gym and looked in the other direction purposefully avoiding it. I hate that place now too. Everything that reminded me of that night, I now hate.

Left turns.

Food-Mart Plus was bustling this Tuesday afternoon. Walking into the newest grocery store in town that had been hyped up for months made me irritated. Everywhere I turned greeters smiled. The grand opening was an extravaganza, free hotdogs, live music in the parking lot, and coupons galore. Balloons and samples were everywhere, and the cleanliness made for surprise reflections, and I caught glimpses of my pitiful self around every corner.

I had meant to get in there to see what all the fuss was about but hadn't made it in, then the accident happened. Everyone I walked past was excited, their smiles annoyed me because I felt obligated to return the gesture. The newness made me aggravated as it was a reminder that my old self would have thoroughly enjoyed exploring the isles and the endcaps. The me before would have shamelessly indulged in every sample offered but not now. I was here for him; I wasn't able to go to his real memorial so I would make my own.

This was a yearning, my brain and heart agreed on this that there should be some kind of ceremony. My attempt for closure and I owed it to David to tell him properly how I felt.

This was risky making a grocery store run. I wasn't ready for people to meet this version of me. People that look like me end up with viral internet pictures and bad memes. They get into fights. *God, please don't let me see anyone.*

God knows I am an overshare-er, but no one wants to know how I'm doing. They either want everything to be pretty on the surface or want the ugly details. It's only natural to have curiosity but they want to feast on the gossip. I was the prey, served up on a platter for other people's amusements. Maybe I was just paranoid but it's what it felt like.

I made a beeline straight towards the florist area. God granted me two things. The first small miracle was I did not see anyone I knew.

This was my quest to honor a man I didn't know. The journey to tell him how I felt about causing his death and this store was my mountain. A personal memorial may seem noble, but my inner voice reminded me, I am not the hero of my tale but the villain.

The second answered prayer was I would find what I was looking for even though I didn't exactly know what "it" was. I was hoping I would just know when I saw it. Once I found it, I hoped I could afford it. I read every card before I found the perfect one. It had blank pages where I could write something. The bonus was a dozen yellow roses that had already fully opened that were on clearance.

"I need 3 white balloons, please. Wait, how much are the balloons?" *I wanted one for each of his children so they would know someone was thinking of them.*

"They are $1.99 each plus tax, what color did you say, white?" I nodded to the busy lady from behind the counter and she responded with her head down working hard on a Homecoming mum. Mums are serious business here in Texas. The bigger, the blingier, the gaudier-the better. It's a rite of passage for a high school girl in the South.

"Oh, well then just one white one please." The balloons were going to cost more than the roses, that wasn't logical. I could justify $2 to my financially stressed husband but not $6. That would be excessive to spend $6 on balloons, totally unreasonable. But everything was unreasonable, I killed their dad, they don't care about a balloon. David is gone, he won't care about my makeshift memorial, but I wanted it anyway.

Internally I was negotiating the cost of everything and if it was worth the argument with Keith. The fact that this was even an issue made me burn in anger, the helplessness of it all. If the school had not been so shady with Keith's contract, we would not be so financially stretched. But I stuffed down my feelings about that, there was no energy to spare. And after what I have done to another family, how dare I be mad? So, I made my little budget work.

"Do you have a sharpie?" She promptly complied by placing the marker in front of me but again diligently carried on attending to the layers of alternating folded ribbon. This mum was growing in exponential size as I stood finding my words. Must have been on a time constraint because I barely existed to her, and that was perfectly fine by me.

I wrote a prayer for the man on one side of the balloon and a letter to his children on the other. "Are you ok?" Her question startled me from the level of concentration it took to simply write legibly on this damn balloon. It was funny she noticed my crying because I had not realized the transition from a few tears to a sobbing mess.

I nodded that I was fine with no explanation as to why I was sobbing, and I handed back the marker.

"Can I just pay for it here?" My voice was shaky.

"Yes ma'am of course," now she was attentive. I unfolded wadded-up dollars and exact change and placed it on the high counter.

Quest one complete. Now onto the hardest climb I had ever faced, going back to the site alone. I wished for an invisible cloak to make it back to the car unnoticed and for the guts to face that hill.

Pulling out of the store parking lot I hit a snag in my plan when it dawned on me the direction towards the accident scene meant turning left. I yielded to a nearly empty four lanes of traffic. There were maybe three cars in this intersection, and I was paralyzed with fear. Instinctively my mind wanted to protect me from the same mistake of not seeing an approaching car. I realized a simple left turn would never be the same.

I gripped the wheel and looked right, looked left, *"I think I am clear, am I?"* Looked right again and left again. Panic started to build. I saw a car turning out further ahead of me, I can make it, no better wait till they pass. Tears began to well and spill and overwhelming fear left me rendered helpless. The car behind me honked and I jumped. They reversed, clearly agitated by my hesitation to go when it was clear. They pulled around me and mouthed the word idiot.

I didn't know what to do. *A voice told me, you shouldn't be on the roads, you aren't safe. Maybe you should call Keith to come to get you.*

Feeling defeated, I almost put myself in park, blocking the exit. Keith would be here in a heartbeat to rescue me, but I switched my blinker to signal right instead.

"I'll just go the long way around," and the click-click, click-click to turn right was unusually loud. I could hear my heart pounding and my loud breathing returned. My senses heightened, highly aware of every car and every possible danger were jumping out at me. I steered where it felt most safe, I had to go right to go left. I added a couple of minutes to my drive to avoid making the left turn. I felt stupid. The next left turn was unavoidable but somehow God gave me the strength to face the hill.

•••

Have you ever walked through the consequences of your actions and felt Psalm 23 in your soul? Like you are walking straight towards what will be the end of you? That's what it was like making the next left turn up the hill. Psalm 23:4, "Even though I walk through the valley of the shadow of death, I will fear no evil, for you are with me; your rod and your staff, they comfort me."

This was another verse I learned early in my discovering scripture as a child. I didn't know what it meant other than death but as a ten-year-old, I found it comforting. David by no means was my enemy but returning to the scene was facing the table so-to-speak.

LEFT TURN, LIFE UNIMAGINED

The table is peaceful, a place of reconciliation. These are essential to healing.

A time to mourn.

My mother tells stories of my stubbornness, a notorious strong-willed firstborn. From the time I could talk, I insisted on doing things on my own, obnoxiously independent. If I was afraid of something, it made me want to conquer it. Fear meant it had power over me, and I would get madder at the fear than the thing I was afraid of. Maybe the stubborn nature of my youth helped me to drive that hill, maybe it was plain stupidity, or a guardian angel going before me? Perhaps a combination of it all. I had never been so scared in my life to take that left turn back up the hill toward the oak tree, but I did.

In the distance, I saw a red car paused at that same stop sign I was at just a few days ago. I held my breath bracing that something might happen. Maybe this time it would be me that crashed. Patiently the car yielded the right of way, as it should. It was still some distance off, then they turned towards me, I closed my eyes and sucked in my breath through my teeth. Nothing happened, the sedan safely passed me on my left. I exhaled a sigh of relief and revelation that nothing happened.

Did he see me, and I just didn't see him? I refocused my attention to the old oak tree and the stop sign. I held my breath and started counting the seconds, one, two, three, four...five seconds to pass the tree, the gate, I was here. Imagining what he saw the last few seconds before we collided. It took 5 seconds.

I can't explain what prompted me to begin counting. I have never felt the urge to do this before. It would now become a habit when passing a stop sign or yielding to stop signs, or waiting for people to pass me. One, two, three, four, five, six...six *seconds to pass me that time. The* voice in my head would count. I was desperate for answers, still trying to calculate the time and the speed.

LEFT TURN, LIFE UNIMAGINED

This two-lane country road had a wide shoulder of pasture on both sides. I pulled off the road and parked in some brush, the opposite ditch from that night.

Why did you not swerve right David? Would this have been different? There are clear 100 yards of grass just right there. Why God? It all happened so fast. It isn't your fault David, it's mine.

The hinge screeched as I carefully opened the metal door of this old chevy to slide down on wobbly legs. Unsure of where I was stepping. I mean who does this? Willingly returns to the scene of their trauma and so soon? Again, the tug of war and back and forth of inner dialogue. I was sure this is what I wanted but unsure that this decision was wise or even healthy. This idea popped into my head a little over an hour ago and I just did it spontaneously. Other people's opinions didn't concern me, not even Keith's. I didn't pray about it, just had a feeling, and went for it. No turning back regardless of my fears. For a brief moment, I stood with eyes clenched before I got the courage to cross the road. I felt the wind of a car drive by. I looked down at the road and saw the paint, still just as bright as it was before. I saw the spot where his glasses laid on the asphalt near the double yellow stripes. I jumped back, a bit startled. Which made me visualize the dangling headlight from his bike. They won't be there when I reopen my eyes.

Crossing the road to the white fence made more sense than standing in the middle of the road. I picked the closest spot to where it happened. Taking those steps was not as scary as the left turn coming up the hill. The blind spots were still very real from both sides however, it wasn't the blind spots that made me nervous. The orange spray paint gave me more anxiety than the potential of an oncoming car. I shrugged at the idea of imminent danger, either I make it across, or I don't. I wasn't testing fate or God but rather accepting the consequences. If it's my time, it won't matter anyway.

Things were different from that night or even from when I visited with mom. Freshly mowed grass, I could tell that someone had trimmed back the branches from the oak tree. I lingered by the fence post before scattering some of the rose petals that were wilted. Gently I propped the bouquet against the fence and stepped back. *What should I say?* How to begin my graveside service? I stood there trying to think about what ministers say at funerals. What should I do? I didn't know any of his life accomplishments or have any warm sentiments or humorous memories to share. So, I just stood, silent. Singing something felt appropriate but there wasn't a song that came to mind. Prayer also felt customary but that didn't fit. *I just want to tell him I'm sorry. Can I do that?* The breeze washed over me, and I felt moved to speak. The slight chill sent goosebumps over my body, it rolled over me, and out came the pouring of my soul. For a second, I wondered if David's spirit had come to meet me there? Maybe he wanted to hear what I had to say. *This is crazy to think about but maybe?*

I tied my single balloon to the fence post and had a full-on conversation with the man from the road. He feels close here somehow. *Can I think of these things as a Christian?* Coarse grass crunched under my feet as I shifted my weight back and forth. I held onto the fence, searching for a spot that wasn't rusted, and braced myself. My voice was nervous.

"These are for you." I looked up to a clear blue sky. *Lord, please give me the words.*

I stood in the ditch next to the road, spilling my tears on dead grass, my should-haves, my excuses, and my overwhelming regret that this was the outcome. I wanted so desperately to connect with anything of David, grasping for some semblance of closure. I meant every stuttered word and sobbed tear that fell from my eyes and dripped from my nose. The apology was genuine, yet it wasn't enough. Words, tears, and balloons were not enough. The yellow roses were not my penitence. Nothing of my own power would be enough. Nothing of human capacity made sense. On this side of heaven, things would never feel right.

I'm so confused; some of these thoughts do not line up with my beliefs. I felt them anyway. Deep down inside my spirit, I knew his soul was in heaven; this gave me great peace. I don't know how I knew but I did.

David, are you ok? Of course, you are probably better than ok. I would take this back if I could. I wouldn't have sent that text, I would have stuck with the plan. Do you hate me for not seeing you? I hate me enough for the both of us. I guess there is no hate in heaven. Is that where you are, heaven? I am so sorry, you probably thought I saw you. I am so sorry I didn't. Why did you not swerve to the right in the grass? You might not have hurt your head like that. I held your hand; did you feel me? I didn't want you to give up or feel alone. I am so sorry this happened. I prayed harder than I ever have in my whole life. Did you hear me? I am so sorry God did not answer my prayer. I don't know what to do now. I feel lost. I am praying for your kids; I know they probably hate me too. I would never have done this on purpose; I am just so sorry...

Only a few cars passed by on the two-lane road. I wonder what they thought driving by as I stood next to someone's property fence and talked to the October sky? Did they know what happened here? Did they mistake me for a family member? What if his family came up here while I was there? What would I do, what would I say to them?

I snapped a picture before leaving. I felt like if I couldn't visit a gravesite, at least I would have this picture; it was a lovely day. When I got home, I said nothing of what I did or said. It was ours, the man from the accident and mine.

❖❖❖

James 1:6, "But let him ask in faith, with no doubt, for he who doubts is like a wave of the sea driven and tossed by the wind." This verse was frequently quoted by my youth minister. It was always in his back pocket of favorite imagery at youth group. He would warn about doubting God's promises, or the double-minded actions that will steal your sense of security. Here I stood 20 years later from those youth sermons doubting my faith and who I was as a person. Sure enough, feeling exactly like the ship tossed by waves at sea. Psychologically being beaten up of my own doing and at risk of drowning in sorrow. Remembering who I was and whose I was would be the anchor of safety to riding out this storm.

No coincidences.

The call I had anticipated from Officer Kurt came later that day. He had some questions, a formality for the investigation. Each simple question tugged the energy meter down a notch. Of course, I wanted to comply but there were some questions I just did not have an answer to. Like exactly how far out from the road did I yield, how far did I pull out before entering the lane, was my blinker on?

"Was anything different that day?"

I wasn't sure how much detail he needed, so I was an open book. Whether he wanted it or not, he got a step-by-step rundown of my day.

"No sir, I taught a class. We had dinner and then went to the volleyball game. But my boys had swim practice, so I left Brooklynn with a friend and drove to the YMCA. The new one in town, not the old one. I worked out on the elliptical (by the weight rack), and then I got a text that my friend had to swing by home. I offered to come to get Brooklynn instead of her getting back out. I went to get her, and then we left," my voice faded because he knew what came next.

"That's good, you can stop there. How many hours of sleep did you have the night before?"

"I'm sorry I don't know exactly but normally we go to sleep between 10-11p.m. and we wake up at 6:30 a.m. for school, so maybe 7.5-ish."

"Were you distracted by anything in the backseat? Were the kids fighting?"

"No, I was just listening to Brooklynn tell me about her day."

"Any arguments with your spouse or anyone else?"

"No, everything was great, it was a really good day till the accident," my voice cracked, and tears spilled out.

"That's all I have, for now, thank you for your time. I will be back in touch."

"Yes sir"

"One last thing, will you be obtaining legal counsel?"

"Yes, I think so, I have an appointment soon to meet with Frank Strawn."

The trembling spell had to run its course before I had the strength to face my family. Sometimes these episodes lasted a couple of minutes, sometimes longer. Regardless, I was done for the day. I retreated to my bed.

•••

Not that I needed a good excuse to skip the last part of a data analysis meeting, but on a Friday afternoon, I did skip it. I finally made an appointment that I was embarrassed to type on my, "Request for Time Off." I marked it as "personal." I was meeting the attorney I had heard so much about. A criminal defense attorney and apparently, he was the best. Does that mean he helps criminals get away with crimes? I don't understand but here I am to hope the skills and expertise will help me. When I pulled up to one of the loveliest landmarks of our historic town square, I realized that I never noticed what businesses were housed in these old buildings. There was a real estate firm, the Lake Hills visitor's bureau, and sandwiched between, the attorney's office.

I always admired the century-old stonework and wood craftsmanship of these offices situated off the square. I just never paid close attention to the signs. I have probably strolled right past it on walks several times and never thought that someday I would need to walk in and receive a free consultation. The Strawn & Strawn Attorney at Law sign hangs just under an iron awning like what you would see in a black and white western movie, it squeaked in the wind. Walking into the office the door was unusually heavy, I had to give it a good tug to pull it open. I thought about all the people who have sought refuge for their alleged crimes here. He has a reputation of being "the best" in town. Some were innocent, some guilty, and few a mix of both. I feel like I land in the "it's complicated" category.

Like a new patient at the doctor's office, my leg would not stop thumping as I sat filling out the clipboard of information. A nervous patient expecting a grim diagnosis. I thought about what led me to this particular attorney. The line, "How did you hear about our office," made me chuckle. I filed in Dr. Paul Knox's name in the blank next to, who can we thank for this referral? He was the first person to mention Frank Strawn. As a child, I only remember being sent to the principal's office once. Dr. Nathan Adams had me wait on a wood bench for an uncomfortable amount of time to hinder becoming a repeat offender.

I am a strong believer that when something happens in repetition, it isn't a coincidence but a divine sign. By "sign" I don't mean mystical witchcraft but divine as in God was dropping a nudge. God has a way of giving you hints and then confirming that hint with a nudge. After the third person mentioned him, it was more like a bop on the head. Everyone who I trusted pointed to this firm. The name of Frank Strawn was brought up from that first meltdown session with Dr. Knox. His words, "If I were in trouble, I would seek counsel from Strawn," have stuck. Since then, I have heard it two more times.

There has been so much to process. It's mostly a blur. There was the accident and his passing, not sleeping, several conversations with law enforcement, a newspaper article, a nervous breakdown, that was just the first week. And now I am facing a Grand Jury hearing, a possible indictment, costly therapy, and a civil suit. The last few weeks felt like I was watching someone else's life play out, someone else's nightmare.

⋯

The phone buzzed and the screen flashed, "Insurance Agent Office " the voice was not my normal representative. The woman's voice was gentle with tone. "Mrs. Anderson, I have been assigned to your case. I am so sorry this has happened, how are you holding up?"

She spoke to me like it was "normal" the way I felt, she knew more about what I was going through than I did. She acknowledged that it was to be expected that I was adjusting to a new normal. She explained she handles these types of claims full-time. There's a department dedicated to this? Her job is only to help people through a fatal crash. The insurance agent meets counselor, meets social worker, knowledge of the laws and workings of the justice system and that's what she does every day. The heaviness of her job I couldn't fathom. Her kindness touched me as she explained the family had secured legal representation, which was standard. She put me at ease as she explained. "I understand," I lied, I didn't understand. Despite the softness of her tone as the listening continued, I had trouble receiving all the information. "We sent flowers and a card… Wrongful death lawsuit depending on the outcome of grand jury decision or trial. Have you secured legal counsel?"

This question was becoming a more pressing matter.

"There is a Frank Strawn near you that comes with great reviews. If you'd like, I can compile a list of defense attorneys in your area?"

That was all I caught from our five-minute phone call. The agent asked me, "do you have any questions?" Stunned by all that she had said I froze, "no, thank you, not at the moment." Truthfully, I had many questions but none that I was able to articulate.

Lord, I need a download of your peace and understanding. This is too much. What should I do next? Please, Jesus, bring the right people in my path. Send me some hope! I don't know if I am deserving of hope but please have mercy. I need a burning bush showing the way to which attorney, a neon sign. I'm not asking for a rainbow to lead the way but total confidence in this decision would be nice. Lord, and can you send someone that knew him, so I can tell them how sorry I am? Please

LEFT TURN, LIFE UNIMAGINED

protect his children, supernaturally provide above their every need, or want. I love you, Jesus, Amen.

❖❖❖

I dropped off the boys at the YMCA for swim practice. There was no way around it with Keith's schedule, yet I could not bring myself to go inside. I avoided anything that I could that reminded me of that night. I thought, I will never eat another taco for the rest of my life. I consciously parked on the opposite side of the parking lot from where I was that night. Now I pull into the closest spot to the entrance which happens to be handicap parking, I hate people who do this. I let the boys out and watch them go in. A family we knew from Hazel's preschool came walking up. I had to give myself a pep talk. *You need to smile and say hi, no questions. Just be cordial, I told myself. Don't say anything about the accident.*

I knew this family as an acquaintance, the dad was a popular personal injury lawyer in town. They also have four children, so it inducts you into a "bigger family" club. Hazel squealed and could not wait to say hi to her friend Hadley.

Every weekday I tell myself this is the day I take her back to school. We haven't unenrolled her, but we haven't dropped her off either. It's like ripping off a band-aid. But then I imagine her telling her friends about our family business. Pre-Ker's are notorious for sharing things that should not be shared. When girls her age are coloring hearts and flowers, mine will be drawing bleeding bodies and ambulances. It's fine, it's Pre-K, she'll be fine. It's only a foundational year of learning social interactions and reading preparedness. My teacher's heart felt negligent, and my momma's heart felt guilt, but still, I wasn't ready. I rolled down the window so the girls could giggle and chit chat. I made small talk until the conversation took a shocking turn.

Hazel announced to her sweet little friend, "My mommy sent a man to heaven!" She said this proudly. Her words choked me, literally sucked the air from my lungs. In her innocence, she was just stating facts, mortified I didn't know how to respond. I was overcome with emotion and began to shake uncontrollably. Thankfully, little Hadley did not understand Hazel's announcement, but the dad, his eyes grew soft. He had heard about the accident; our small town does not keep secrets. As I fought back tears, he gave me the name of a man named Strawn, an attorney friend that he recommended.

"Jenna, I would call Frank Strawn the best guy for your situation. I'm so sorry," he said genuinely.

"Thank you," trying to hold it together, I rolled up the window. He picked up Hadley and she waved us goodbye. We retreated home. I could not scold my four-year-old for her blurting out a very private matter. She needed to process this death as much as I did and in her way. To her heaven was a good thing. Why would I tell her otherwise?

Out of the mouths of babes. What was my daughter's perception of me? How will this affect her as she gets older when she realizes the truth that I hurt a family? In the coming days, Hazel brought me pictures of the accident. The man in the road is bleeding but smiling. The first time this happened I was shocked how many details were drawn out in bright orange marker. She would point to the ambulance, the lights, the bystanders, the people who knelt around the man, "this one is you mommy, and this is the man you hurt." "He went to heaven Mommy!" She assured me he was in heaven; she was adamant. We were always smiling. She made sure to include the blood and tears but always smiling.

There is a part of me that is glad she is expressing herself, impressed by the realistic features of the drawings. These aren't the scribbles of a typical preschooler, it's easy to distinguish what she remembered. Our car had a steering wheel, his motorcycle on its side. The ambulance had lights.

LEFT TURN, LIFE UNIMAGINED

I thank her for sharing the picture with me and it kills me. With shaky hands, I receive them and stick them in a drawer in the nightstand to give to the counselor.

Free consultations.

The tinkling of a chime from the heavy wood door at the attorney's office snapped me back to reality, a man delivering a package glanced in my direction.

I looked down, embarrassed to be seen here but glad to be back from my daydreaming. I had many people they could thank for the referral. I knew with absolute certainty this was the right place.

Folded neatly in my purse was a short list of questions. *Will I go to jail? What are my possible charges and what does that mean? How much does your representation cost?* An extremely important detail because I wasn't sure we could afford him. *When will I know if I will be arrested or not? If I am arrested, how do I make bail? What exactly is bail? How much will bail be? How is it ok for the paper to publish an article when the crash report isn't released?*

I nervously placed the completed clipboard on the receptionist's desk, and a kind older woman came forward from a long hallway. She greeted me with a gentle smile. I am sure I looked as pitiful as I felt.

"I'm Mrs. Strawn, his secretary," she said. She motioned me from the lobby to a consulting room that smelled of cedar furniture and cinnamon. She had a demeanor that invited calm, empathy, and I felt the need to collapse in her arms and sob.

"Do you need anything? Would you like water or coffee?" She put me at ease as she handed me cold bottled water draped in a napkin and looked over the packet making sure everything was complete.

Mr. Strawn had almost the complete opposite first impression. When the town-trusted attorney did come in, he was every bit lawyer-esk. Don't get me wrong he was tough in tone, to the point, no BS, he did in fact wear an eye patch like a pirate. I could tell he was a man of his word; he looked straight through me with his one good eye. He glanced over my explanation of why I was there and got down to business. I was not prepared for his questions. Was this a consultation or rapid-fire mini-trial practice? Sensitivity wasn't why anyone hired him. If he is like this in his consultation, I can only imagine his charisma to command a courtroom. He led me through a series of questions to get a better idea of the mess I was in. He listened intently and clarified facts, timelines, etc. I could barely make it through a response intelligibly. I was a sobbing mess and trying to keep up. Then when he was satisfied, he paused to think, and I was able to catch my breath.

"Now Jenna, you got to stop beating yourself up," he said confidently. He had a choice to get on that bike without a helmet. We live in a world with risks."

"But from what I am hearing, you are not criminally negligent here. You had an accident." You are civilly responsible, yes, no doubt. Your insurance will help you with that part or let them know I am willing to represent you in those matters as well. But on the criminal side I feel confident we have this nailed down."

"You weren't drinking, you weren't speeding, you weren't on your phone, putting on makeup, you weren't eating or engaged in sexual activity."

"No, sir." I nodded in agreement to each of his statements and continued to wipe my tears with the tissue his wife offered me. I took a couple, but she left the box. I felt as if when he listened to me, he didn't see me, but someone like a daughter. I felt that comfortable. And I knew that Mr. Strawn was a godsend.

"What's the Legion? "I asked awkwardly. After all that he said and all the many things I rehearsed to ask, this question was not on my list. The list was out the window.

"A restaurant for Veterans, I would bet that's where he was headed, that's the only thing on that road. I frequent there myself. They have a great steak."

"He was a Veteran?" I sobbed.

He wrapped up the consultation with the disclosures of there are no certainties, each Grand Jury takes on its own personality, but I think this will end how we expect it to.

"Are you seeing a counselor?" He asked. I told him, yes and the girls too. He gave me two analogies that captured my attention. The first was he compared a car to a loaded weapon and license to kill, people don't use caution as they should. Why had I never thought about it that way before? The other statement was something like, had this been a two-car collision, damages, and injuries if any would be minor. Another fact I had never thought about until now. We all have parts to play in every scenario. We all have choices and there is a risk all around us. These words of wisdom spoke to my logical brain that had checked out. The logical thinking had been taken over by an emotional downpour and that part of the brain was exhausted.

I knew that I knew that I knew, deep in my spirit, that Frank Strawn would be the best person to represent me. I didn't want or need a second opinion. The first thing I did when I got back in the car was call my mom. "Momma, we have to hire him, they agreed to work with me on their fee, he is the one."

"We will find a way," she assured me.

As soon as the call ended, I was overcome with a feeling that maybe I should just turn myself over and not fight. Maybe I deserved punishment and should plead guilty. Mr. Strawn's pep-talk and assurance had already been drowned out by negative voices. How can I fight for my innocence when I feel so guilty? How will we pay for this retainer? Look what I have done to hurt my family, how selfish, look what I have done to their family! I took their daddy! I'm driving a loaded weapon; I don't want to drive anymore. I don't want to hurt anyone else.

I shook off the thoughts as best I could to get home. I put the feelings of doubt and fear each in their own designated box in my mind. A visual technique for when I can't deal with everything. I imagine this shelf in a storeroom in my mind that is collecting boxes of emotions. I know they are there; I even feel like it is somewhat organized there. I can't let them out, not all at once and not for when I need to make the eight-minute drive home. I can do this, I said to myself. While I was in the office it must have rained on our side of town or it was some kind of miracle because, in the distance, there was a small half rainbow popping out from behind a cloud. I felt God put that rainbow in the sky just for me. I smiled and it almost instantly began to fade. It was just a bright spot, a wink from God.

∴

The truth of the Gospel is simple, your Father in heaven loves you. He gave his son Jesus for you, me, and every other person on the planet. We are loved beyond measure. A pure unconditional love. When we believe in him and declare him Lord over our life, he dwells in us. Romans 8:1-2, "So now there is no condemnation for those who belong to Christ Jesus. And because you belong to him, the power of the life-giving Spirit has freed you from the power of sin that leads to death." I held on to shame and guilt because I felt it was my penance. Contradicting all of God's word. Accepting his grace takes trust in him, releasing how the world sees me or us from our failures. Bars or no bars, sentence or clear of charges; there is no condemnation in Christ Jesus. If you feel anything other than that truth, there is work to be done in your heart.

Love is persistent.

Later that night as the kids were all asleep, I whispered to Keith, "I am going to start selling things to pay for Mr. Strawn this weekend. I think some people from church are going to give me things too. And mom and dad said they would help."

"We'll do whatever it takes," Keith assured me.

"Unless we go to trial, I'll probably just take a plea deal. He said it could cost $30-40,000 dollars for a trial. I won't do that to us."

"Yes, we will!" He said adamantly louder than a whisper.

"Shh, you'll wake them up! Let's hope everyone sleeps through the night."

He pulled me in closer to him, "If you weren't on the other side of the bed, I wouldn't have to whisper so loud." He said it was kind of flirty. I got tense thinking about intimacy. I wasn't ready to be flirty, or to be held, which broke my heart. He did nothing wrong. I didn't know how to explain that when I close my eyes, I see a bleeding man in the road. It wouldn't be fair to either of us, he would be making love to me, and I would be subconsciously locked into my trauma. So, I pulled back.

I am drifting farther from my old self. The me before would have melted with the line, "Come closer let me whisper in your ear." He sensed my tension and let out a big sigh. I've built a wall to self-preserve and shut out the very thing I need the most, love, human touch.

"When can I have you back? I miss you," he said painfully. His quarterback-sized hand cupped my cheek.

"I don't know but I am trying," and the tears gathered in his palm.

I woke to the sound of the kids downstairs and my eyes opened to the smells that were floating up.

LEFT TURN, LIFE UNIMAGINED

I had all intentions of getting up, going through items, and sorting what was worth anything to sell. We needed $2500 for my retainer, which felt like it might as well be $25,000. But I lay there not doing anything but staring. The kids didn't disturb me, but they tried their hardest to make the downstairs life more appealing than the security of an isolated bedroom.

I heard the TV playing a familiar movie, I smelled maple bacon which aroused my curiosity, but I couldn't bring myself to move.

Keith came upstairs with a plate of my breakfast favorites, French toast, bacon, a couple of sliced peaches sprinkled with cinnamon, and a coffee frothed to perfection.

"Want to eat up here or I can bring it back down if you want to join us. The kids are playing. I think it would be good for you to come down."

"This looks amazing thank you, can you put it on the dresser?" He set it down.

"The kids made up a new game, they've been playing well together all morning. They want to show you. They kill me with their imagination."

He said kill me, why did he say kill me?

"Look at them, they're so silly," he sat beside me and laughed at his own video of the kids playing this game. "They named it Beater Ball. A mix of soccer, hockey, and quidditch from Harry Potter."

"It looks like fun, sounds like they are having fun. I'm sure the whole neighborhood can tell they are having fun."

He brought the video to show me the life I was missing, yet I barely blinked or smiled. His face was disheartened with my comment. He looked defeated that the bacon, and the coffee, and the kids playing, and all the effort wasn't enough for me to rejoin my family and the life we had together.

"Babe, I don't know what to do. What do you need? Are you depressed, sad, is there something I can do?"

"I don't know, maybe y'all are better off without me, I could go live with my parents until this is all over."

"No, that's not an option we need you. The kids need you and I need you."

I didn't respond so we just sat in this space. I laid on the bed curled up and he sat on the edge of the bed making his best attempt to connect with his wife.

"Please stop blaming yourself." His voice cracked but he swallowed it down.

"Please don't tell me it was just an accident," I couldn't take that phrase one more time.

He let me be.

•••

I've gotten good about shutting out the world, both to the outside world and in our home. The cell phone stays on silent, and I watch it light up and vibrate. I stare and ignore. People need things from me I can't give, like conversations.

"Pick up your dang phone!" Her text was practically screaming at me. It was Anna, a friend who was more like a sister. We've been friends since August of '91. I wore a crimped side ponytail and a blue jean vest for my first ride on bus number 7. I was all freckles and braces then. Definitely not one of the cool kids. She let me sit next to her.

We had moved two weeks into the new school year but within the same school district. This meant a new bus, a new route, and the stressful task of finding someone willing to share a pleather seat. Seats defined social status. Every seat was filled or claimed, "taken."

I made my way back to the front feeling desperate when Anna looked up at me. She was sitting in the middle. This communicates she didn't plan on scooting or sharing but her mercy saved me from having to sit right behind the driver. Now that I know her, this gesture was painfully annoying. I can just imagine her thinking,

LEFT TURN, LIFE UNIMAGINED

"Fine, sit here but don't talk." To break the few minutes of silence I blurted out the oddest question, "Have you ever worn a pad before?" A hot taboo topic for tween girls. Anna rolled her eyes at my immature question; she was a 6th grader, and I was in 5th grade.

"Of course, I have."

We've been friends ever since. As my maid of honor, moments before we opened the church doors for the service to begin, she whispered, "It's not too late if you want to escape. I will drive you anywhere you want to go." And she would have taken me anywhere in her cherry red Civic. Vegas, Mexico, anywhere. I need only say the word. When I looked her straight in her hazel eyes and said, "Nope I want to marry Keith." She proudly met me at the altar, fluffed my train, straightened my veil, and held my bouquet with tears in her eyes ruining her eyeliner.

"I will keep texting you and calling you, so answer the dang phone!" I knew it was true, she'd drive to my house to pull my butt out of bed in the most loving way. I gave in and hit the call back button.

"Hey"

"Hey you," she quipped back! "Decline my call? You know better than that!"

I think I grunted so she did what any protective friend would do, she checked in on the basics.

"Have you showered?" She got right to the self-care questions to which I replied no or with an exaggerated truth.

"Have you put on clothes?"

"Pajamas are clothes."

"But have you eaten?"

"Keith just brought me a nice breakfast."

"Jenna Lynn, you are nasty, it's time to get out of that bed and wash your face, and brush your teeth. You will feel better. Get the stink off."

"Anna, I am hiring a criminal defense attorney, I am preparing for my life in prison.," I said this jokingly.

"Girl, they make you shower in prison. A guard will be like, 'you have 5 minutes ladies,' and if you refuse, they'll hose you down."

My laughter turned to tears and even though she couldn't see them, she knew they were there.

"I got the girls in to see the counselor. Anna, how screwed up am I going to make my kids?"

"Screwed up enough. How is Keith taking all of this?"

"Keith is amazing. I don't know how food keeps happening but here we are in football season when he is really busy and poof food keeps appearing."

"So, what you are telling me is the kids aren't starving."

"Yes."

"Well good, glad I don't need to call CPS on you." she laughed.

I laughed. "Love you, Anna!" She is one of the only people in the world who can make me laugh in an existential crisis.

"This session is free but next time I'm charging, just kidding. Love you too, go take care of yourself, people love you. Don't forget that!"

"Awe, you got all mushy."

She is the definition of the phrase ride or die, if I go to jail, Anna will come to visit me and have an escape route planned. Just kidding, kind of.

♦♦♦

Proverbs 17:17, "A friend loves at all times, and a brother is born for adversity." Carrying each other's burdens and standing in the gap for people in prayer is not a suggestion but a mandate. Sometimes we will need to be carried on a mat to the feet of Jesus by our friends and family. Other times we will be the ones carrying a friend. This is an honor and a privilege. I struggled at times to ask for help, I wasn't always honest about just how bad I was dealing with the sadness. I thank God every day for the community God gave me and I look for opportunities to pay that forward. If you have been set free, share the good news and be a friend, we never know what someone is dealing with. Give the gift of presence.

Sleep past the pain.

Sensitive chapter, trigger warning suicidal ideation & self-harm.

If and when I came downstairs, it was out of absolute necessity. My presence caused a disturbance that made me sadder, therefore I avoided it. I could lay upstairs and drift to happier times without interruption. Like when we road tripped to Canada with a whole basketball team. We ate a famous Philly cheesesteak from the original Steve's Prince of Steaks. I was taken back to random memories. Watching the sunset on a cruise ship as a senior class chaperone, or even nursing my babies to sleep sitting in my grandmother's rocking chair.

I entertained anything besides the present reality. I would relive childhood memories like playing under a willow tree, riding my powder blue bike past my designated area, or going to Disneyland or cheering at high school football games. Reminiscing the glory days would produce a smile and blank staring at the wall. Memories take me away. But my favorite pastime was still seeing Keith and me at the gym right before the accident. I would make up alternative scenarios than the one that played out. If only I could control my sleep, keep it peaceful, happy, where I write the storyline and happy endings. Dreaming of what I think should have happened.

Keith let me know that dinner was served. This man kept inviting me to join the land of the living, our family. God bless his tenacity. Sometimes his invites are endearing, other times aggravating because I just want to be alone with my thoughts. If I stay distant maybe that will be an easier transition if I am gone. But this time I remembered Anna's encouragement and followed him downstairs.

Pasta is both low effort and cheap, we have served some form of the simple carbohydrate five meals out of the past week since our budget has become even tighter. We are in a rotation of hamburger mac, tuna mac, spaghetti, or ramen. Tonight's dinner is a bowl of off-brand mac & cheese, the powder-kind with cut-up hotdogs and a side of steamed broccoli. My appetite was as sporadic as my mood swings. Keith offered me some wine with my pasta, but I declined, "No thank you." The bottle in the back of the fridge had gone undisturbed. I could drink the whole bottle and it wouldn't take the edge off. Grateful the Holy Spirit took that desire from me. Before the accident, I usually enjoyed a cup of coffee in the morning and a chilled glass of sweet wine before bed. Neither had happened since the accident.

Caffeine in any form magnifies the discomfort in my chest, heart palpitations only make me spiral into thinking, this is it, here comes the time where my heart gives out. But it keeps on beating.

I need someone to shake me firmly by the shoulders. Wake me up inside, tell me what to do and how to feel. If I could just get some sleep? Maybe I could function a little better. The intrusive voices in my head were so loud it was hard to drown them out. White noise was no match for the inner dialogue. I would toss and turn through the night, then I felt guilty for disturbing Keith. I watched him breathe to remember to breathe. I exhaled when he exhaled. Some nights I would talk to the man on the motorcycle, and he would ask me, "Why did you pull out in front of me?" Sometimes he would tell me about heaven, sometimes I would replay the scene, and this time he would sit up and be okay. He would stand up, dust himself off, and everyone would cheer.

Frustrated from staring into the dark, I quietly slipped out of bed and into the bathroom. *I need to sleep more than 2 hours! You know what is ridiculous, $800 worth of damage the claims adjuster told me earlier in the day. Eight hundred dollars and a man's life. I couldn't stop thinking about his words. Surely, he didn't read the memos of the gravity of my case?*

"I have good news," he said, "Only $800 worth of damage to your car."

What can I take? What can I take to stop thinking about the agent's voice? He was smiling when he said it. I shuffled to a medicine basket recounting the conversation that disrupted tonight's sleep. I felt like I was in a fight. I wish I would have told him where to put his, "good news."

A lot more damage was done, I wanted to scream. This is the level of damage you can't assign money with. I felt nauseous, I began to panic. Here we go, I felt the clamminess set in, my chest grew tight. My heart was bursting at the seams with all the feelings. I wish I could just unzip my chest and let everything spill out. It would be so nice to tap out, surrender the white flag.

I longed for restful sleep that would make it better. If I just knew they were okay, that would make it better.

The lavender oil a friend gave me diffusing by my bed wasn't strong enough. What about another melatonin? I dug through the catch-all medicine basket and found a nighttime pain reliever.

"PM Pain reliever," I wish. I felt the need to shoot the finger at the bottle. I rolled the bottle around in the palm of my hands. I briefly slipped to a dangerous place of thought. I just want to sleep and not wake up until the pain is gone. I wanted to sleep and believe this wasn't true. I wanted to just rest in nothingness, no feelings or dreams, no voices, or thoughts, just rest.

"How many can I take to sleep past the pain?" Even my spirit was startled by the thought, and I put both bottles back in the basket and hoisted it up to the top shelf, pushing the dust from unreached places to trickle down the cabinet door.

God, you promised that if I came to you, you would give me rest. There is no rest in my soul, Lord. Where's your unfailing love now? I feel like you've failed me. God, I can hardly breathe, please help me to breathe. I paused my prayer to struggle to breathe in all the way.

LEFT TURN, LIFE UNIMAGINED

Thank you for that breath, thank you for normal breathing. Help me, Lord! I hid at the top of the stairs to not wake anyone, when I felt the panic dissipate, I returned to bed.

That was a wake-up call to how deep I was in my depression. Consider me officially shook. I returned to my damp pillow, my heart racing. My pulse skyrocketed and I could hear the swooshing of my heart pumping in my ears. These thoughts left me helpless, and I was so afraid to tell anyone what they whispered. This was a new level of rock bottom. It's like I hit a floor and then the earth opens up and swallows me up and I land on a new level of rock-bottom, and it happens again and again.

The next morning, I moved through the motions exhausted from the internal fight through the night. And the daylight did not bring reprieve. The fight just continued with new contenders. Tell someone about my thoughts that scared me, or just keep praying for them to go away. Stay in my room where it feels safe or escape and face the real world. Thus far I've stayed in my room, and it hasn't served me. It's "ours" but lately it feels less like mine and Keith's bedroom and more as a hideout for my depression.

Because I rarely left, my family started to come to me. Hazel had dolls and colors she played with as I laid there. She entertained herself on our bed. The kids would make pallets, even family board games took place on the floor of our bedroom. I would occasionally engage with a comment or laugh but from my pillow.

This was not healthy, and I was present enough to know how unhealthy it was psychologically and emotionally to live life confined to four beige walls. I felt guilty for that too. I was at odds with myself and tired of fighting. I was ready to surrender. I cannot go on like this! I just didn't know who I would forfeit to. I have two logical options, I could fight to make some good come from this tragedy, but how? Or not fight, give in to the sadness. This is no kind of life. I would teach a class and return to my bed until it was time to teach again. Weighing my options, fight or give up, fight, or give up, I was contemplating how long I could keep surviving in this headspace. *Just get through today, maybe the answers will come tomorrow.*

How long can a person go without sleep? What is survivable? Whatever is minimal for survival because that is where I'm at. Food had no taste, there was no desire to laugh or be intimate, all I did was cry. Imagine a life without joy again, without restful sleep? Without feeling worthy of love or life. What kind of life is that? A sad one. Would my family miss me? They already miss me. I am not the person they love; she died too that day. Maybe not physically gone but everything else of substance needed a resurrection in my life. *Lord, I'm dying, I need a miracle in me. A jolt of hope.*

The voices would catch me when I felt most vulnerable. "They are better off without you." This thought played on a continuous loop. *Was I depressed or just overwhelmingly sad?* Brain fog clouded perceptions of tone and facial expressions, nothing felt as it did before the accident. I was trapped within me. Bound with chains that I forged and shackled myself. I was a slave to my self-loathing. Isolation is heavy like a weighted blanket but not the cozy kind, a suffocating one.

The voices and thoughts that plagued me didn't feel like they were mine, I felt tormented. Dare I admit this turmoil is almost demonic. I became paranoid everywhere I turned. I wondered who was talking about me, who was uncomfortable with my presence, who knew David's family? Was someone plotting against me? Constantly on edge.

I just wish I could sleep past the pain was the repetitive thought that I battled. Convinced sleep would make it all better.

⁂

When we are overcome with temptation, God's word says he will provide a way out. We must work for our healing, humble ourselves and resist the devil and he will flee. 1 Corinthians 10:13, "No temptation has overtaken you that is not common to man. God is faithful, and he will not let you be tempted beyond your ability, but with the temptation, he will also provide the way of escape that you may be able to endure."

There is no special sauce to this or secret power, the choices I had during the aftermath of the accident. I still have today. We must resist, fight the good fight, and never give up hope. Miracles are birthed from dark places; we must hold on.

Love unconditional.

I knew this was not the life I wanted. I believed there had to be some good still in me because I cared what thoughts like these would do to the people that loved me. Thank God there was not a little megaphone attached to my brain announcing all this mess. There was still a little warrior in me after all the scrambling and sorting the thoughts trying to label what was good, bad, real, and exaggerated. This battle was serious enough it scared me into action. I didn't stop praying until sunrise. I knew I needed help to see this through for the long haul.

The next morning, I was unusually thirsty, dehydrated from crying most of the night. So parched my lips were cracked. My nose was raw and red and puffy. My throat was dry, leaving a sticky paste in my mouth. It coated my tongue.

"Can someone bring me some water, please?" I tried to yell but my voice was hoarse. I heard them laughing at the television.

"Hello," I called down again. Can anyone hear me?" I needed a glass of water, but no one heard me. I tried to ignore the urge for water, but I could not shake it. Finally, I surrendered and headed downstairs. Before I reached the bottom, I was greeted by my family who were partaking in a family tradition without me. "Mom, are you coming to watch with us?"

I'm so thankful they did not hear me calling, I would have missed this. Thinking about it stings my eyes with gratitude because the next few moments, I believe changed the course I was headed.

They were all huddled together watching the Charlie Brown and the Great Pumpkin Patch movie, we watch it every year.

"I came down for some water." Without prompting, Asher, my tender-hearted son, sprung up to fetch a glass eager to please me. The rest of the bunch all scooted over to make room for me almost in unison. "Mom please stay and watch with us. We don't want you to miss it!" But what they were asking was please don't leave us! Their facial expressions pleaded, don't go back upstairs. Their eyes begged me to stay, stay just as you are. Their love for me ran deep and despite all the enemy's lies, it was evident that their hope for me had not run dry.

They were the water my soul needed; their unconditional love was like an unexpected encounter with Jesus at the well. I was fully wanted despite my faults, I was loved. If I needed a reason to fight for hope, these were five. As painful as this was, I didn't want to leave them. I didn't know how to find my way back or if that was even possible, but I would not give in to my hopelessness. That moment was what I needed.

God forgive me. You can't win any more Satan, you can't take anything else, get out of my head! I feel like there is a whole army of demons poking and prodding me. If you are here God, I need help, I need back up. Please show yourself in this, I need light out of this darkness. Jesus, help me. I need hope, I need help.

Thank God my secret affair with mental illness remained mostly private. I sat there next to my babies, watching this cartoon about hope and perseverance. The tears fell. I was snuggled in, surrounded by unconditional love. I kissed the top of Hazel and Asher's head, each leaning in against my shoulders and hope sparked inside. Hazel gave me a smile that scrunched her nose. She leaned her head in and took a deep whiff of my armpits.

"Mom, you smell delicious," she declared.

"Do they now?" I laughed.

"Gross, did she just smell your armpit?" Connor winced at the thought of Hazel smelling my body odor.

"What, they smell good to me. I love mommy's smell, she smells good!" She defended herself to her older brother. We all laughed. I smiled appreciating the sentiment.

"You nursed her too long Mom! Hazel, that's disgusting!"

"She's four, and she loves her momma, stinky armpits and all!" She nodded. This precious child would crawl back in the womb if I let her. She always wants to be in my lap, on my hip, or in my personal bubble. I used to joke that she was an endless supply of snuggles like she had to get them all in and make up for being the last born. Hazel was our rainbow baby. Named after my grandmother, Tommizelle. Some people called her Tommie, others nicknamed her Hazel, but I knew her as Nana. Our Hazel has her carefree spirit, for sure my most affectionate child, and she completed our family perfectly.

Every time I thought about her smelling my armpit, I let out a genuine belly laugh. The gesture was strangely sweet. "You are so silly," I tapped her little nose looking up at me! Her bright eyes blinked tears of joy. Hazel was moved to tears because I came downstairs. My heart swelled; her unconditional love pierced me. As the kids enjoyed the movie, I silently prayed for more guidance. I did not know how to climb my way out of this grave. The good news is the walls had not caved in on me. There were glistening eyes all around. Even Keith looked hopeful I stayed. He stretched out his arms draping them around Hazel, reaching the back of my neck. He gently massaged it. I caught him more than once glancing over at me, he wasn't thinking about pumpkins or the crowd on the couch. I felt his talks with the Lord. I don't know what was said, I have some ideas, but he was genuinely happy to have his family together.

Negative self-talk is poison. I was drinking it up, choking it back. A dark lonely place, a pit. Parts of you feel that the pit is where you belong. You don't see the way out, and no one knows how far gone you are. You lie about how bad you feel to protect your loved ones as if ignorance is a cure. I know I have to get these thoughts under control.

There was no manual or self-help book for taking another person's life. I searched and searched, longing to find hope in other people's situations similar to mine. It's a black hole of a topic. No one talks about causing an accidental death, and I understand why. But surely people heal from these tragedies?

Once again, sleep felt impossible. I had hoped with such a wonderful day and budding outlook, things would be different.

"Jenna, it won't happen overnight," I lovingly told myself. This time I avoided my bathroom. The medicine basket would beckon me. It lied and said it held a solution to my sleep troubles.

The sleepless nights can't have power over me anymore, it was time to take a stand. I am taking back my power. If I wanted to remember who I was, I needed to find her in the things I did before the accident.

I quietly grabbed my Bible and notebook and snuck away to the floor of my closet. It's been a while since my last prayer-closet session. I was overdue. Post-it notes that lined the wall next to hanging clothes had verses for healing and prayers for Hazel. It was time to wipe the dust off and set up camp in my secret place. For many months this space had just been a closet, but there was a time or two, or three where this is how I battled. It was a retreat, a quiet place, where I could hide and have an encounter with the Lord. The time read 1:36 a.m., "Psalm 136 it is."

"Give thanks to the Lord, for he is good." I paused to hum a song based on this verse. "His love endures forever."

Are you good, Lord? I know deep down that you are. Does love endure this?

Verse 23 and 24 hit home. I want so much to return to how I felt before the accident.

Seek my nature, return to me. The thought made me emotional.

With only a plain notebook, the teacher in me came out. I needed to sort my thoughts. I folded a clean page to make a crisp crease down the middle and opened back up the paper. On the left side of the fold, I scribbled- God is/truths. On the right side I wrote, lies from the enemy.

God is good.
God is love.
God forgives all sin if we confess it.
He sees all sin the same.
He is my comfort.
He will never leave me.

I wrote every phrase, truth, and promise I had grown to believe over my years as a Christ-follower. I stared at the words and reread them. I believed these to be true with my whole heart up until the moment of the accident. On the right side of the crease, I wrote every belief I had about the enemy of my soul.

Satan is a liar.
He is a thief that steals, kills, and destroys.
He is the tempter.
He is bondage.

I made a list of thoughts that had tormented me. The evidence was clear that the voice I heard and the feelings I felt were not from God. God was not the enemy. I would keep this thought organizer with me by my side and in my purse at all times for weeks. I would look at it to filter each thought. It felt good to spend time with God in this way. There are times when you feel compelled to devour the Word and now was one of those times. I opened my Bible and went to work using my post-notes to write out all my favorite scriptures down. I stuck these notes everywhere. On my nightstand read, 2 Corinthians 12:9 "My grace is sufficient." I can look at it and know he gives me what I need for each day, just one day at a time. Just make it through the day. I even thought about taking a sharpie and writing, "His grace is sufficient," on my forearm in case I forgot.

Still, I could barely stand to look at my reflection, so on the bathroom mirror, I would read 2 Corinthians 4:16-17, a reminder to not lose heart. Even though I could not see it, God was working day by day. I didn't understand the how, but I trusted the words it stood on. Psalm 62:8 near my desk to speak to me when voices call me to my bed instead of facing my day. Above the visor, a yellow post-it read Joshua 1:9, where I felt most vulnerable, and the fear was suffocating. Reminding me to be strong and courageous. Placing God's Word scattered around helped me feel protected. I didn't know if it would help, but it certainly couldn't hurt.

Along with the scriptures, I decided the silence was unhealthy, so I replaced it with praise and worship music. Everywhere I was, there would be worship and hymns playing in the background. I found the negative voices drowned out by the music and scripture. I was also talking to the Lord about anything and everything, it's hard to tear your soul apart while talking to God.

I sent Dr. Knox a text the next morning:

"May I make an appointment with you? I am also making an appointment with my regular doctor."

Dr. Knox responded almost instantly: "I am available, when are you?"

He was available. That's so nice of him. He might be a living angel; this man truly has a servant's heart. I knew that if I did my part to get healthy, God would use the people in my life to help me along the way.

Dear God, help me to remember who I am. Thank you Lord that you are here. This feels good like a step in the right direction. Protect the steps Lord, guide me. Lord, please comfort his kids. I hope they are okay. Please God provide for them and for us. Lord help me to have hope, I am so tired of fighting for hope. Lord, please help me to meet someone that knows him. I need them to know my heart. Help me to meet someone like me so I know I am not alone.

I am here with you, I felt him say deep inside my being. I am here with you, I felt it again. I felt him again. This thought made me smile.

◆◆◆

When you don't know what else to do you can call on the name of the Lord. You praise Him in desperation. Replacing the negative with God's word was a game-changer for me in this time of sorrow. It didn't change the circumstance, but it did, however, influence my perception. A crazy thing happens when you pursue the Lord with your whole heart, the desire to know more grows. You find yourself getting lost in scriptures, smiling as the words come alive. I inserted my name in the scriptures and remembered that the promises of the Bible included me. This led to praying for others. I began to press in with praying for other people's requests, praying for miracles and breakthroughs to refocus energy into something positive. This energy awakened my soul.

The power of prayer.

Weeks before the accident Brooklynn was selected to pray for the One Nation Under God Conference. We were nearing the 2016 elections. She was given the specific task to lift up her generation. Four people were selected from a tri-county, nearly forty church collaboration. Of all the possible youth she was asked to pray in front of the thousands that would gather at our town square. I can't tell you how excited and proud we all were when she got the invitation, but now I was secretly worried they chose the wrong family. Of all the families that love Jesus in our area, our daughter was chosen and during a season like this. If people knew what we were battling, maybe they would regret their decision. Not the wrong member, Brooklynn has been a prayer warrior from toddlerhood, but us? We were all so broken, including my daughter. She saw things she should have never witnessed at twelve years old.

A rehearsal was scheduled a couple of days before the event. This required leaving the house because Keith was working, so I had a "Come to Jesus" moment in the mirror before I drove her to the meeting. I looked at my reflection and gave myself a stern talking to while brushing my teeth. I had one of these talks with myself a couple of times before, just not on this level.

At the end of my sophomore year of high school, a boy from the youth group caught my attention and my heart. By Junior year, I lost myself to the intoxication of first love. I found myself caught up in an abusive and controlling relationship. I had many mirror moments pleading with my common sense to have the courage to break it off. As a young mom of three babies in diapers, I found myself disconnected and blah. I was resentful and bitter, especially towards my husband. I lost my joy under a cloud of Postpartum Depression. I was suffering and had no idea how to ask for help or admit the monster I was to my family. There were many intimate conversations in the bathroom. Through tears, I would remind myself of the things I had overcome, and it would happen again. And now here I am again, an accidental killer, who didn't want to be this person.

You know you can't keep living like this. It's time to stop wallowing. Fake it till you make it. You know what you believe, you believe in forgiveness and mercy, and for dang sure not an eye for an eye. You believe in miracles and answered prayers, and grace, so act like it. Do it for David and do it for the four kids that depend on you. Do it because Keith still believes in you and mom and dad will never understand the goodness of God if you give up. Take yourself in that church, and God will do the rest. Just smile and nod and wave. You don't have to answer questions. Show your daughter that what people think doesn't define you.

The worship band was practicing an Elevation song called "Holy Spirit You are Welcome Here," and I was drawn to hum along. The speakers were gathered in the back to pray together for the event and for each other. I squeezed Brooklynn and kissed her forehead before she scurried off to join them and I looked for a place to lay low. A friend's mom that I regard as a mentor, Mrs. Sandee grabbed my hand as I was passing by. I planned to sit in the back pew, but she stopped me. The shame in me made me shrink back startled by her touch. I hoped to go unnoticed, but she saw me. I imagine the Holy Spirit pointed me out as the one afflicted, the lost sheep desperate to hide in the crowd. She had heard about the accident and sought me out to speak a Word over me. Her gentle touch was ministry, and I'm certain her presence scared the demons I battled.

I broke down in tears with just the touch of her hand like she transferred some peace, I was too ashamed to look her in the eyes. She lifted my chin and said, "You are a child of God Jenna, God is not your enemy, and he loves you. Only the enemy comes to steal, kill, and destroy. God is not your enemy," she repeated. "You are not abandoned nor forsaken. He is here, he is inside you, he is in your marriage, and he is in your children. *She pointed towards Brooklynn.* God sees the pain you are in, and he hears your heart, he is right here with you. He told me to find you. Look at me, God is good, and he is for you don't ever doubt that."

I felt her words wash over me and I could breathe. Her hands were now holding mine and something supernatural began to warm them. It felt like we held light between our palms. Her thin fingers clasped mine tightly and she shook them with emphasis with each bold statement.

"This is not His plan for your life, this accident was not your purpose but what you do with it can be. You are going to come through this. The only way out is through." She spoke these words with complete confidence like she knew something I didn't. Tears streamed down my cheeks, and I felt the comfort of the Holy Spirit like a blanket of love and light. Her prayer wrapped around me like a cocoon. Mrs. Sandee is an angel who walks the earth. She loves the Lord passionately, it's hard to describe her nature because she is so rare and everything I would like to be when I grow up. Kind, gentle, meek but bold, and humble, generous with her wisdom and knowledge, and transparent with her life experiences.

I am forever grateful for her obedience at that moment to speak life to the parts of me that were dying. She was the hands and feet of Jesus that day. Her prayer and the praise band were oxygen for my spiritual lungs and a transfusion of hope for my soul.

The least of these.

The week before the 2016 Presidential election felt like the country was anticipating some monumental change. There was a bustling momentum towards election day. People came in droves; all the surrounding counties came together; it was as close to a jubilee rival as I had ever been a part of.

It was estimated a couple thousand people stood in agreement, all praying for the nation that day. The idea was to pray for peace, pray for the next administration, pray for God's will. In the sea of people that stretched out as far as you could see. I wondered if his family was here too. Would anyone want to hurt my daughter or boo if they recognized our name from the paper? Fears melted when Brooklynn took the stage. Her twelve-year-old frame looked so small on the big screen until she began to speak. The anointing transformed her; she was bigger and bolder, not at all a shy little girl. I have never seen her in this light before. Where does she get that courage from?

Her prayer was powerful, and her words ministered to all who listened. None of it was what we did as her parents but the Holy Spirit that flowed through her. With barely a quiver in her voice, she spoke fire, and the heat reached the crowd as they cheered in agreement. She proclaimed the truth of God's promises. "Young or old, he has a purpose for your life," she declared. "God loves you, and me and every single one of us just as you are," she exclaimed. My daughter was ministering to me. "God's word says he knew you in your mother's womb. He designed you for a purpose according to his will. God only wants us to believe in him and surrender our lives, our pain, our plans to him. All sins can be washed away." She declared generations to renew their relationship with the Lord. She prayed for the unborn and the lawmakers. She prayed for protection over children and that the young leaders would rise up. She proclaimed unity in our nation, wisdom over voting, and healing in our homes. She was as broken as we all were, but that could not stop the strength of the Lord shining through her.

I felt alive again. I was in awe again. We are the least of these, the people who you would least suspect to be used to share hope or deemed least qualified. There was no doubt Brooklynn was called for this very moment. People in the crowds listened to my baby girl and wept. She was the youngest to pray that night. No one would have guessed the heartbreak of our family, the trials we have faced and the valleys we were currently walking. No one knows the pain she endures. They didn't know she had been vomiting from nightmares at night and none of that mattered. She was the willing vessel, and the Holy Spirit did the rest.

Brooklynn's story.

Brooklyn has spent every day of her young life in excruciating pain. The doctors said she likely suffered spinal headaches because she has a complete spinal fluid blockage. We never knew. She still smiled, and played, and carried on as a happy little girl. The fact that I know how she suffers makes this more remarkable. We can all learn from her. I can choose to smile and carry on too.

When I was pregnant, my spirit knew she was a girl. In the days leading to her birth, I read the entire New Testament. I prayed like crazy. I was in a season where I could not get enough time with the Lord. I found myself completely immersed in seeking God. Looking back, God was preparing me. Brooklynn would be a warrior, and as her mother, I needed to be equipped.

Her testimony began at just a few weeks old when she had the first sonogram of her spine. She had a spina bifida dimple, and doctors could not guarantee she would walk. As she hit her milestones like a champ, the worry began to fade, but a little after her third birthday, she would have neurosurgery. Brooklynn has Chiari malformation and she developed a syrinx in her spinal cord. Doctors prepared us that she might need to learn to walk again, talk again, potty train again, and may require multiple surgeries. But no, this little firecracker fought us to wear a diaper in the ICU. "I'm a big girl, mama. I don't want a diaper!" She yelled at the nurse and shook her head at me with tears rolling down her cheeks. Her feistiness made my heart smile, her fight gave me hope. Chasing her through a children's hospital on a tricycle with bandages stapled to her head gave me strength. I had no choice but to keep up.

Her love for Jesus has always been unique. When she was little, I could never keep a nativity set complete; the baby Jesus was always missing. The case of the missing Jesus was eventually discovered. Brooklynn had gathered them all up and kept them safe under her pillow. She tucked them in and kissed the porcelain pieces at night, that's how she was found out. I heard her talking to the baby Jesus.

At age five she was afflicted with abdominal migraines and cyclic vomiting that stole her sleep but not her joy. At seven she prayed her baby sister into existence and Hazel was born five years to the day of Brooklynn's brain surgery.

To see her now I stood in awe. This can only be the work of God. She knows and feels him on a level all her own, a personal relationship with Jesus. Every parent's prayer. My hands reached out in agreement; she was no longer just my daughter but a sister-in-Christ. I lifted my hand higher and whether I said it out loud or not I am not certain, "Praise you, God! This accident did not steal her faith, the accident does not have the last word over her life! Thank you, God!" and I cried with pride and hope and gratefulness. I was so glad I was here to see this moment, what if I had given up? *Oh God, I thank you.*

•••

I will never forget her on that stage. I almost did not let her participate in fear that she would be booed or slandered due to my actions. The Lord uses young people to do incredible things. I watched my daughter with great faith in her small body. She was the example to us all of what God can do with an offering of courage. She didn't focus on the crowd or our circumstances, she simply showed up and gave God the platform to use her. As time has passed, I have used this moment to encourage myself in whatever task laid ahead. I have also reminded my daughter of the twelve-year-old self that she can do great things, unimaginable things when she lets go of the fear and trusts God to meet her. Jeremiah 1:7-8, "The Lord replied, "Don't say, 'I'm too young,' for you must go wherever I send you and say whatever I tell you. And don't be afraid of the people, for I will be with you and will protect you. I, the Lord, have spoken!" Each of us can be used for the kingdom of God all he needs is a willing heart.

Baby steps.

The couch was less scary this visit, with Dr. Knox. He was a reliable source of peace. He answered every text and every question with honesty and compassion. While I waited, I thought about which fire I wanted Dr. Knox's help putting out first.

Keith was aggravated that I was tired from the prayer rally. Since the accident, I have had to be wise with my energy. It was depleted easier and would often take longer to recover.

His patience was wearing thin. He needed some hope too. He needed assurance that I was making an effort to have some sense of normal.

"How long will you beat yourself up like this?" he asked me.

"I don't know; what's an adequate time to bounce back after killing someone? A month? A year? You tell me, who gives me permission to move on?" My sarcasm wasn't helpful, and I knew what he meant. It was like I could see the apple on the tree, it was right before me. I was hungry for the apple, and it looked good. I knew it was sweet and would satisfy me. If it was out of reach, people would provide a ladder, or turn over a bucket and lend me a hand, but I refused. There were people on hands and knees, willing to bend over and make a step with their very own back and yet I just looked at the apple dangling ripe in the branch.

"I'm sorry, I don't know what is wrong with me. I have made another appointment with Dr. Knox. I'm trying; just everything feels like an obstacle."

How can I explain what I am experiencing if I don't understand myself? Every second of every minute since October 4th, I have thought about the accident, I see David's face, and I'm tortured by the fact that I don't know if his children are okay.

Staying in my room is a form of self-protection. Downstairs even on good days, it was a circus. The daily grind of motherhood becomes overstimulating now. Bombarding of needs that I simply could not withstand. I used to joke that I would hear my name, at a minimum, one hundred times before noon. I didn't want to blow up because I couldn't meet their needs. Everyone needed a piece of me, and I had nothing to give. But I missed the questions, I missed the ability to multitask, and I missed handling them with grace. I missed my circus.

•••

"Sorry about the wait, Jenna. Good to see you. Glad you called."

"I don't know where to begin, Dr. Knox I am not okay. I feel angry."

We just began to pull back the layers and put out fires one by one. I was reaching for fruit. From cuss words, to safe sleep aids, the importance of self-care, to managing driving anxiety.

"Do you remember any dreams?" he asked.

I nodded.

"What do you see?"

"Most of the time I am at the stop sign, and I am trying to watch for his motorcycle coming over the hill." I can never see him, but I know he is there, so I just wait. I feel the rumble of his Harley, so I wait, and I don't pull out of the subdivision. The worst one is that I am about to leave the house and when I go outside there are people there. Shouting and chanting, holding signs and stones, telling me I should be in jail. "Share the road," they chant. I just fall to my knees, stretch out my arms and take it. Sometimes I am in the middle of the road looking over David laying there on the pavement. He opens his eyes and looks at me, looks straight through me, and asks me why I pulled out. Sometimes he opens his eyes and smiles. He says not to worry.

Saying this out loud, the dreams and the delusions, took the edge off, exposing them from the shadows of my mind and freed space to think more clearly.

"I think it's normal for what you are feeling, it's a normal response for an abnormal situation," he said kindly.

He assured me that what I was describing was PTSD (Post Traumatic Stress Disorder) symptoms.

Grace, do I deserve grace? Grace is for when you forget to call someone back. Grace is for when you were 10 and put a candy bar in your pocket only for your parents to make you later return and pay for it. Grace is for when you snap at your spouse after being up all night with a gassy baby. Or forget to move the laundry from the washer to the dryer. Is there grace for this?

My grace is sufficient. I heard God say to me.

I told him about my notebook and how I write down my thoughts.

"Keith and I had our first argument."

A couple of days ago I got a call from him that enraged me. Keith had been at a job site in Hidden Lake Estates. Dr. Knox sat straighter in his chair. I immediately became guarded that he was there, I didn't want to think about that place. It felt like a betrayal that he went there, and I didn't know.

"Babe, I was there at the stop sign, I don't understand how you didn't see him. I saw plenty of cars coming over the hill." Feeling shocked at what he was insinuating, words and air escaped me replaced with a burning. "I am shorter than you and the car sits way lower than your truck. I don't know what to tell you."

He thought of that, so his next move was to get out of the truck and sit down next to the road.

"Are you kidding me?" I screamed. "You sat on the road?" I hung up on him.

When Keith got home later that evening, we avoided eye contact. You could cut the tension in the air.

"Why don't you just leave and take the kids while you can and have a normal life?"

"I've never seen you like this babe. I don't know how to help you, but I am not going anywhere."

This man is loyal to his core, loyal to a fault. He really would go down with the ship, I am the ship.

"Dr. Knox, are we prolonging the inevitable?" The look on his face after airing it all out, he knew we needed some support, and fast. He listened intently and nodded sympathetically. "Maybe next session Keith could join us," he suggested.

"How will I ever make him proud again Dr. Knox? How can I be an honorable wife? I just don't know how we can make it through this."

My sessions with Dr. Knox felt helpful but I could not share everything. Dr. Knox was a safe place for many topics, but hearing strange voices and intimacy were not. I would hold on to these secrets a little longer. He gave me an assignment before our next session.

"I want y'all to get out of the house, go camping, take a walk, be together as a family in the fresh air and next time we will bring Keith along to have a joint session."

Whatever Dr. Knox suggested I would do, so I planned a weekend getaway to East Texas. Maybe the trees have changed colors, maybe my mother-in-law will make her homemade cinnamon rolls and maybe I won't feel pressure or guilt to take care of everyone for a couple of days.

November 1, 2016.

Dear David,

It's been four Tuesdays since it happened. My brain can't wrap my head around it. They are doing a benefit dinner for your family for the one-month anniversary. I want to go but I don't want to hurt anyone. I asked some friends to go in my place. I am praying for a great turnout. I am sorry for all this; I don't have a better word than sorry. There are a million little things I am sorry for. Sorry isn't good enough. Will you forgive me? I asked God to tell you I stopped at the stop sign, and I don't understand why I didn't see you. I am so very sorry I didn't. I pray for your children every day, multiple times a day. I am sure you are watching over them. I hope that they are surrounded by love and comfort. I hope they feel that you are near, and God is near. We are taking our family to get away, I will think of you. I don't know how to live anymore, David. Is it ok to use your name? I see it everywhere now and I don't know if it's a sign or a curse. I know we aren't friends, but I held your hand. I did everything I could, did you know that was me? I don't know if it is ok to be happy or to try and be like the person I was before the accident. I don't even know how to be the person I was before the accident. I was a nice person, I never wanted to hurt anyone. I will live my life trying to honor your memory. It wasn't supposed to be this way for either of us. Thank God you are at peace, maybe someday this will make sense because right now it doesn't.

So very sorry,
Jenna

More steps.

Desperate times called for desperate measures, and I wanted drugs, the pharmaceutical kind. Surely there was a man-made chemical solution: to be happy, be awake, help me concentrate, stabilize my mood, and nervous system, and for the love of God help me sleep. My prayers for healing weren't being answered, turning to medical science was the next right thing. I was hoping to leave the appointment with a remedy for all the woes.

At the doctor's office, I filled out a clipboard of papers the receptionist handed me. The need to "update my file from the last appointment," made me snicker a little. Reason for the visit, give me all the drugs, is what I thought but I wrote, annual checkup. Pap smears are never anyone's favorite, but I needed a happy pill and Dr. Brad is the only person I have discussed depression with before. I was due for a physical, so here I was hoping for a miracle drug to solve my mental problems and make me normal again.

Dr. Brad Benson makes you feel comfortable and supported, his southern gentle charm is just a bonus. He delivered our youngest son Asher, a healthy 7lb 8oz boy nearly ten years ago. He was familiar with my stubborn will as I labored 18 hours without an epidural. He supported my choice. He has already seen me through hard labor, silent tears of confirmed miscarriage, and he was safe to talk to about all subjects including sex. This man was also a witness and recipient of the most embarrassing moment of my life. Legs spread in the glory of labor stirrups; I passed gas directly in the man's face. He was gently stitching me up after giving birth to Asher, such unfortunate timing. I almost died.

"I am so sorry Dr. Brad, please forgive me!" completely humiliated.

"It's why we wear the mask," he laughed. It's a miracle I can still look this man in the face, but he made it okay.

My husband still loves to tell the kids that story. This is the same doctor that helped me with postpartum depression. With a list of questions to discuss including the topic of intimacy, it was folded neatly in my pocket in case I forgot what to bring up. Which is what happened, I forgot all my questions. I blanked out about it once I undressed and hopped up on the examination table. I scooted my bottom and the white translucent paper stuck to my butt cheeks. The funny thing is I was about to get more vulnerable than I already was. When he asked, "How have you been?" While I sat half-naked on the cold crinkly white paper, he wasn't prepared for the floodgates to open. His sweet nurse clung to my side as I cried and recapped the last few weeks.

My sweet doctor asked, "tell me what's been going on." and so I did. With sobs and stutters, uncontrollable shaking, I told him what had happened.

"There was an accident" I sobbed. "I hit a motorcyclist, his name was David, he was a father, a Veteran who served our country and he died because of me. And it was all my fault, and I can't sleep, I can't eat, I can't feel and it's just so horrible. I am so horrible. I might have to go to prison, can you believe that?"

They both just stared blankly with compassion without saying a word.

"At my six weeks appointment after having Asher and we talked about the symptoms of Post Postpartum Depression. You asked if you could do anything you enjoy right now, would you be ready and excited to do it? I answered no, I kind of feel like that now but worse." "Nothing feels good at all. I just wish I could crawl in a hole and sleep and not feel this. I think I am going crazy." My head dropped to my hands, I felt their hands on my shoulder to remind me they were there and that it was okay to let go.

"You aren't going crazy, Jenna, you are grieving," he assured me.

This is grief? Grieving a stranger, I never thought about how to label the emotions. I thought this was depression. It's a little of both.

This was the first time I acknowledged my grief. A part of me was lost that night in October. When I've tried to explain these feelings, I was met with a myriad of responses, most of which no one could understand my layers of feelings.

Maybe I was overdramatic, selfish, or crazy. How could I feel like I had experienced a significant loss? Although I did not know him there was an entanglement of our souls. That brief moment may have been one of the most significant in both our lives. He forgave a stranger and passed to glory, I received grace, and the beauty of the cross came alive. Before we had help at the scene, the operator asked me if he was breathing. I got down really close to watch for movement in his chest but all he did was let out a long smooth exhale. That may have been the last breath he took on his own. I am honored to have been there to hold his hand.

When I finished pouring my heart out, something remarkable happened. Dr. Brad on my right and Nurse Karen on my left, we were all in tears. Peace filled the room. They listened with no judgment, just compassion and then he said something I will never forget.

"For as long as I can remember I have had a recurring nightmare since I was about nineteen. I have dreamt that a young child runs out in front of my car, and I am unable to save them. It just pops up and it's terrifying."

"I am so sorry if you relive that over and over, I know what that feels like." A miracle happened. Without hesitation I asked him if I could pray with him, and he agreed.

So, there we were in room 5 sitting bare bottom on the table, in my open back cotton gown and the sheet draped across my lap, we bowed our heads to pray. I took both their hands in mine, and I prayed for Dr. Brad to be free of this haunting. God could still use someone like me despite my brokenness because I felt him, as real as

Brad and Karen's compassion, the Holy Spirit was there in the room. Now the light was in our hands, and they began to warm just as they did with Mrs. Sandee and countless times before that.

"Lord, I ask that you give Dr. Brad rest from this dream in Jesus' name. You made his hands to heal and to help, and not to harm. Go before him in all things, let nothing the enemy has planned come to fruition. Give him absolute peace and freedom from this dream. We stand that no child or other person will be harmed by him. Send your angels before him in all that he does. Thank you for your life's work and for calling on Dr. Brad's life. We thank you for healing and rest, giving him complete rest from this recurring dream. Guide him in wisdom in all that he does. In Jesus Mighty Name, Amen"

It took us a moment. But just like that we all cleared our throats, wiped our tears, and completed my visit. I'm happy to report all was well in the lady parts. I left his office with a diagnosis of grief and another therapist's name that specializes in PTSD. He wanted me to try and do some of the things I loved. He and Karen would partner with me and follow up regularly. I forgot to ask about intimacy and was too ashamed to admit the thoughts about wanting to just sleep past all this pain. Before leaving Dr. Brad recommended a trusted attorney he knew from the golf club, Frank Strawn, with a sigh of complete gratitude that this was another confirmation I needed from the Lord.

"I have heard he is the best, I plan to hire him."

Before I drove off, I pulled out my notebook from my purse and wrote what he had said so I wouldn't forget.

I sent a text: Dr. Knox when will I feel normal again? My doctor says I am grieving, and he also thinks showing signs of PTSD.

Dr. Knox: Yes, you are. You have a new normal.

Me: We are going to take the kids to East Texas for a little getaway.

Dr. Knox: Excellent! Let me know how it goes.

LEFT TURN, LIFE UNIMAGINED

After dinner, I helped Keith with the dishes. "You know you put bowls where the cups go," I teased. The kids were distracted, I couldn't ignore the tug on my heart any longer. I apologized for hanging up on him the other day and for the curse words I slipped. He began to reciprocate when I said it was okay, "There's no manual for this. Maybe the kids should sleep in their room tonight?" I playfully nudged him with my elbow.

It was an exhausting and wonderful day. Putting terms like PTSD and grief to how I felt gave me hope. I knew what we were dealing with now. I knew how to research to gain understanding, this gave me the tools to advocate to the people around me, and most importantly, I knew how to pray.

"I love you," he said, "we'll live in a cardboard box if we have to as long as we are together." He kissed the top of my head, and I listened to his heartbeat.

"I love you too." The funny thing is I knew he meant it. I pretended to sleep until he started to snore and twitch his arms gently every so often, so I knew he was sound asleep. I just watched and listened without complaint. He inhaled, I inhaled, he exhaled, so I did; the rhythm reminded my body what to do. This became a new normal when he slept. He would breathe, and the sounds would calm my spirit. His breathing sustained my own. I'm so grateful for this man. I always thought we were oil and water, two opposites that attracted. Keith would argue we complement each other's strengths and weaknesses. His strength amazes me but what's funny is he would tell me the same!

I loved to force my eyes to see the shadow of the features of his face and rounded shoulders. Tonight, I talked to him.

"I love you, honey, I really love you," I whispered.

"Thank you for taking care of me, of us, and I am sorry for what we are going through. I am sorry I can't manage to get out of bed or be the woman you fell in love with."

JEN EIKENHORST

Dear God, I don't deserve the love he has shown. This is unconditional love. Please continue to strengthen him. Bless the work of his hands and the steps of his feet. Lighten this financial burden. I know he is weighted down and worried, he has to be. I love him so much, this is more than I deserve. Thank you, God, thank you, thank you for him, for all of them.

Searching for community.

In pursuit of rekindling my faith, it started with the basics. Making prayer a priority throughout my day. Listening to worship and the word of God every opportunity. In my quest to find scriptures to help me with grief and lament I found passages in the Old Testament about Cities of Refuge. Places for people like me, accidental deaths were mentioned in the Bible, and God made a point to address it. To be acknowledged is to be seen, to be seen is to have a voice, and God made sure people like me had something to cling to. Maybe I wasn't, "a killer." The six cities for people to flee to are referenced in the books of Numbers, Deuteronomy, and Joshua. Admittedly, I haven't read the whole Bible cover to cover. I've devoured the New Testament over and over, but the Old Testament just skipped around.

Searching for help on grief is easy, taking steps towards healing takes time and courage. Go to any bookstore or search engine and you will have your fill on books, articles, research, and opinions about grief. Try to find one about accidental death grief, and there is nothing. There is no self-help book for accidentally killing a person. Empty searches felt hopeless and lonely. *Surely, I am not the only one?*

Usually, when someone grieves on this magnitude, everyone around you is also grieving. As hard as my family has tried to understand and the lengths I have gone to try and explain; unless you know, you don't know. They didn't connect with him as I did. They didn't share in my grief in the same way. If anything, they grieved the person I once was.

On an ordinary day and on a whim, I searched, "accident & death & unintentional & fault." The digital sea was parted and found a refuge so to speak.

A website dedicated to accidental or unintentional killers. I could not believe my eyes. An unexplainable joy filled me up and spilled out of my eyes. It was an overflow of happy tears. I wanted to call everyone and shout from the mountain tops, "me too!" These are my people; I've found my people. The founder was like me, except in her case a child was involved. She knew the struggle, she knew the heartache, she coined a term, C.A.D.I. acronym for (Causing Accidental Death or Injury).

The phrase accidental killer made me cringe with shame. It's a cruel label, one I could never bear, but C.A.D.I. is something I could explain with dignity. That's what this website offered, the hope for dignity and community amid a tragic situation. The website had an open forum with hundreds of entries, people from all over the world leaving their story and their guilt in a safe place to confess. I read each of the stories, I knew the author experienced freedom. I wrote my own and I wrote the founder. This was divine, God knew I needed this. A needle in a haystack to find, the only one of its kind in the world, this was a gift. An answer to prayer.

I recognize that it's strange to find a connection with strangers that share your pain, or is it? The fire inside me was joy, pure joy, it was hope-filled, finding The Hyacinth Fellowship stirred the social part of me that had been hiding in the cave, afraid to come out. Afraid to share openly, but these people knew, and it was good. I suddenly felt a little less crazy, slightly less alone, and hope was kindling in my soul.

1 John 4:18 There is no fear in love, but perfect love casts out fear. For fear has to do with punishment, and whoever fears has not been perfected in love. What we love should be evident in our life. This idea of a love list was not a piece of cake. Why is this so hard, I thought? At the root of the issue was trust, do I trust God and his word? Am I worthy to love and be loved? His answer is yes, I need to line up with his eyes!

I love to laugh.

I love the smell of homemade biscuits and honeysuckle and vanilla candles.

I love worship music and 90s R & B.

I love to dance.

I loved painting and writing poetry when I was young.

I love going on bike rides.

I love the ocean.

I love it when Keith and the kids sing.

I love Keith's kisses and his eyes and being wrapped in his arms.

I love my family.

I love you, Jesus.

It's intimidating to call out your fears. I was nervous that the list of things I feared would be double or triple the list of what I love. I was right about the estimate but bringing light to what would rather creep in the darkness of my mind, body and spirit was exactly the problem. It can't live in the secret places of my heart anymore. I was afraid of a wide range of legitimate to absurd and even laughable scenarios. I feared most not having the guts to keep fighting for my mental health and becoming another victim.

I feared causing someone to not believe in God because of my actions. If you want to know how to rip my soul from my body, tell me I caused my brother to stumble or I caused them to disbelieve. That, I cannot live with. I also feared that there was this pending doom on my loved ones, and it would somehow be my fault. Logically, I know this is highly unlikely however, these were the battles, and my number one priority was to seek strategies to combat each and every one. One by one. Truth to conquer the lie. While doing that I would look to engage in the things I loved and hopefully add to that list with time.

Lord, I want to live again and to stop being afraid of everything. You promised you would give me the desires of my heart. If that is true, I desire to love people deeper and experience the fruit of love. I desire a harvest from this drought. Only you could do this because I can't. I just want to be well; I would like to be able to breathe again. I feel like my heart might give out, so heal my heart, please. I want to meet someone like me so I'll know I can make it too. Help me to meet someone who knew him. Then I could tell them how sorry I am and that I am not a horrible person. Lord, I give you every fear, I surrender it to you, and I trust you. Amen

Looking over the list I realized they were all things I haven't experienced in so long, no wonder I felt empty. *Try to do one.* Do one hard thing a day. This is the thing that popular ministers don't preach about, the strength to endure. This will be a choice I make daily, maybe for the rest of my life. I would keep fighting for healing, I was still in the ring. It feels like Round 9 but I'm not tapping out!

Pray for them.

Driving to East Texas has always felt like going home, even though I am a Dallas native. The I-20 highway is lined with walls of red and brown trees. Remanent of the grueling Texas heat and drought this summer. It's mesmerizing going 75 down the highway, there's beauty even in scorched trees. You can always count on the scenic drive to remind you of the Creator. This is why nature was prescribed by Dr. Knox.

We passed through a small town of Athens for a quick bite to eat and to stretch our legs before visiting with family, further east. Just off the exit, there is a little fishery and conservatory with walking trails and wildflowers.

We were out of the house, exploring together. There was the smell of lake water. We followed a gurgling sound that led to where you could feed the fish. Twenty-five cents for a handful of feed. We each got our allotment of quarters and tossed to gluttonous fish. We laughed and gasped at the fish that jumped and splashed fighting over little pellets of fish food.

I'm convinced nature is medicine for the soul because I appreciated every detail. I was out of bed, praising the Lord for the sunshine. This was a Psalm 19 kind of day. "All of it, the heavens declare the glory of God and the work of his hands."

So many things to be thankful for, I was even thankful to be thankful. Yesterday was one month since his passing. Life was still moving forward. No one realized a month had come and gone but me. If they did notice, they said nothing. I talked to David about it. I lit a candle in his honor.

We crossed over an old wooden bridge that made me question its ability to hold us. Keith said, "Nah, it's solid." He bounced up and down and smiled, the kids squealed with nervous laughter. This man of mine has no fear. His playful smile did not prevent me from reaching for the railing for dear life. The drop wasn't more than five feet, but my grip looked otherwise.

With every inhale of fresh air, I was more grateful. With every exhale there was less weight. I *want to breathe you in God and exhale anything, not of you, I thought.* Each cleansing breath was chipping away the walls I had built. It took everything in me to be present. I would find myself drifting to daydreaming, mumbling to myself, talking to God, or to David.

There was energy to smile and freedom to laugh, and the tears were the happy kind.

We approached a clearing; the kids and Keith took off sprinting to a nearby fountain. I felt the itch to chase after them. I didn't run but I thought about it. Watching Keith pretend to let Hazel win made me smile. I moseyed behind, always the caboose of this crazy train. When I approached the fountain, I froze.

There are coincidences in life that make you pause and think, "Isn't that funny?" This was not one of those times. There, engraved on the 5x5 silver plaque was the name of the man in my accident. My mind was surely playing tricks on me, but no. My whole body shook, and my breathing became labored. My heart raced inside a tightly squeezing chest. David Norris Williamson did not seem like a popular name, but again I would have never noticed it pre-accident. I thought maybe this was a hallucination. I had to sit down.

My David, the man who I hurt was named David Norris Wilson. A Veteran from the U.S. Navy, father of three, family man, good friend, survived by his brother. An avid sailor. This is all I know of the man from my accident, just a few personal facts from the obituary in the paper. I struggled to breathe alone on a bench next to the fountain. The family was playing hide and seek in some nearby cottages. I didn't want them to see me like this. I cried and prayed for God to help me breathe. I thanked God for every breath. I told myself, I am safe, everything is okay. I concentrated on the small sounds around me. I heard the fountain bubbling, the kids giggling and shouting, I heard a bird call out. I felt the wood bench, the breeze, I twisted my rings around and around my finger. I looked closer.

"It wasn't his exact name. It belongs to a different person, Jenna." It didn't matter to my brain; the chemical response was in motion and all I could do was ride the wave. A chill came over me, it was the breeze and the emotion, maybe it was an angel or David's spirit, or maybe it was only the November breeze that caused me to shake. I began to cry. I felt powerless over my own body, and that made me angry. I reached out my forefinger to read the silver plate. This fountain was dedicated by the family. It read, in loving memory of David Norris Williamson.

My family called out to ask me if I was coming. I made my way towards them, confused and stunned. Exhausted from the episode. My breathing had almost returned to normal, but my eyes were red and puffy from crying. The mood changed. Energy left me with every weighted step back to the car. I obviously can't escape his name, and it feels like an ambush each time I hear it or see it.

Of all the parks and places to stop in East Texas, we chose this one. Of all the names, one so significant would grasp my attention.

Lord, what do I do?

Pray for them.

"Pray for them?" I responded to the voice in my head. Is that you, Lord? Pray for those that love him. A gentle voice responded to my question.

I will pray for his children every time I hear his name? The idea had come to mind before, but now, I was sure. Keith and the kids were confused as to why my sudden change in behavior. I didn't tell them about the plaque or the panic attack, so they blamed themselves.

"I don't understand what happened, honey. Was it the kids or something I did? The bridge was safe. I didn't mean to scare you."

"It wasn't that." He is blaming himself. But I couldn't bring myself to tell him what I saw. He wouldn't get it anyway. If I admitted I saw his name, he would remark that it's silly to let a name bother me like this. That would have made me upset. There wasn't an easy fix for this situation. Every moment of every day is a Russian roulette of possible triggers. I can't have a plan for an infinite possibility of scenarios, but I can pray every time I hear or see his name. I will not let his name bring shame on my day, it will not cast a shadow on random parts of my life and prayer seemed the only way I knew to combat this little happening.

"I'm better now, we can just move on and enjoy the rest of the day. I closed my eyes, laid my head against the window, and watched the blur of trees. Parts of me wanted to be bitter that the enemy showed up on our day in nature as a family. I could have easily missed the small nameplate but I didn't so it must be for a reason.

I reached for his hand and said, "Honey, I appreciate your patience with me, it was nice to get out."

God, I need your help here.

It started that first night of the accident. I turned to the Bible app for comfort but from every mention of the name David, I would feel a sting. I started reading over his name, just skipping it. My subconscious blubbing over it, made it better. As if it his name was a bad word. But it wasn't bad, I just felt unworthy to speak it. I associated all David's with the David from my accident. I was tempted to put all scriptures with the mention of David away, never to read again. The name David is mentioned over 900 times in the Bible. He was a key player, to avoid his name would mean avoiding scripture altogether.

Just a couple of days after the accident, Hazel asked me to play with her in her playroom, her sweet hand grabbed mine and led the way. I sat down on a cold rug, and she promptly brought me an orange Bible not much bigger than a deck of cards. Just her size, like the ones that street evangelists hand out, no idea where she found it. She curled in my lap and said, "Read to me, Momma." Of all the books we own, she chose this one, and her little fingers turned to a random page with delight. Again, there was his name, David.

I tried to escape it by skipping that chapter but again, five letters that now had power over me. It hurt to say his name. I have thought of his name hundreds of times. David takes up all the blank space in my mind, every day. Like an echo I entertain. Saying his name out loud felt sacred. I was dangerously close to idolatry; all of this was unhealthy. Praying for his children made the most sense. I drew a line in the mental sand. It won't matter where I am or what I am doing, when I see or hear the name David, I will take that as a sign to stop and pray for his family.

Dear David,

I saw a fountain with your name on it, it wasn't yours, but you know what I mean. I decided every time I hear your name I will pray for your children. I hope they are okay! I will do anything for them. Anything! I can't be scared of the name David, you know? I don't feel you would want that, you looked like a nice man. I want to go on with my life and live it, really live because you didn't get to. I'm so sad though. I don't even know how to be me. I don't know how long I can go on like this. I gave your glasses to the officer, they weren't even broken, I hope they make it back to your family. Do you watch over us? I'm sorry. Never mind why would you watch over me, stay with your kids? Heaven is better than here, right? I read in the paper you liked sailing; do you sail in heaven? I'm sorry you didn't get to sail on that trip after you retired. I've never been on a sailboat, but I love the ocean. When I see sailboats, I will think of you and your children. You wouldn't believe how divided we are as a country, the election around the corner. You fought for our country, does it make you proud or sad because of where we are? Ask God for me, why did he let me hurt you? I never would have hurt you, David. Never, not on purpose! I will never understand. People are so angry with me, are you? Do I deserve to be in jail, should I be hurt too? What is fair? I am so sorry. Did you see the sunset tonight? I tried to enjoy it and hoped it was better from your view. I prayed for you and your children. What do I do David, what can I do to make this better?

I rambled for pages with a letter never to be received, a letter to hold all the things I wish I could say.

No one happened to notice the significance of the day except for my broken heart. No one else cared his name was on that memorial fountain, but me, this was my issue.

When I was just a naive sixteen-year-old, I went through a difficult time with friends that had lost their way. Childhood dreams of being kindred-spirits forever changed in high school and it became a very lonely season. My parents were a little concerned, so they arranged for me to visit with two of my favorite Elementary teachers. (Mrs. Hudgens 3rd grade and Mrs. Murphy 5th grade). My dad knew I respected them both as role models. Mrs. Murphy asked me what she would always say to us at the beginning of the day. "Sit up tall, square your shoulders, smile, and do your best." She nodded; this advice applies to all of life. They gave me a light catcher for my window with the Serenity Prayer on it. A stained-glass cardinal perched alone on a branch. The prayer is shown through the sunlight. I kept it in my window near my bed. Often it was the first thing I saw before getting out of bed. Ritually I would pray this simple prayer that God would grant me peace to accept the things I cannot change and courage to face the things I can and wisdom to know the difference.

As I lay in bed waiting for Keith, I journaled what I could control, and I remembered that day and the simplicity of the serenity prayer. Oh Lord, how the words of that prayer ring true now. His name and when I encounter it is out of my power but having a plan that would bring me peace and honor his memory is within my control. God, please give me the wisdom to know the difference.

He emerged from the shower of my mother-in-law's home, the same bathroom he used as a kid. "Overall, it was a good day" he applied an obnoxious amount of toothpaste to his brush. I ignored my temptation to nag that he left the water running at the sink.

"Aside from my freak out, yes it was." I put away my journal and tabled my thoughts about finding David's name at the fountain.

"Honey, have you heard of living organ donation?" he stuck his head out from the bathroom brushing his teeth, not sure where this would go.

"What if I donated part of my liver or a kidney?"

"We aren't going to talk about this right now."

"I am serious."

"Honey, I'm serious, we have had a good day and I am not talking about this right now."

When he came to bed and leaned over to kiss me goodnight I said, "What about being a surrogate? I could give life to a family that can't have a baby."

"Good night, babe." he was irritated.

"Come on, that would be okay, right?" It would be a way of giving back. And if the baby is a boy maybe they would name him David." As soon as I said it I realized how unhealthy this thinking was, clearly I would not make it past the psychological evaluation.

"Honey, I love you but there is nothing you can do to make this better, it was an accident. There isn't an act of atonement, no amount of self-sacrifice or punishment, Jesus did that on the cross, he was the sacrificial lamb. Do you believe Jesus died on the cross for all sins?"

"Yes! But"...

"No but's, that is the beauty of the gospel." Besides if you want to have another baby it should be mine then we would have a full quiver." Ha-ha.

"Full quiver you are crazy you just want your own little Anderson basketball team. We can't afford the ones we have now, and I am even crazier now than I was in my twenties with 3 kids. Thirty-six is no spring chicken."

"And who says you aren't my spring chicken," he kissed me.

"They are pretty amazing kids!" my voice cracked, here came the tears. His handsome grin let out a sigh.

"Good night, babe, let's get some sleep."

"Honey, if I die before you it's okay for you to marry again. Just don't marry someone half our age and have your 5th baby, okay?"

He laughed, "I can't marry some twenty-five-year-old and have my 5th baby?" He laughed.

"No! No, you can't, or I will haunt you." I teased him. "You'll come home, and all your kitchen cabinet doors will be half open and you'll know my spirit is there," I said smiling.

"What if I like that idea of you haunting me." After a long pause, he said, "I probably won't marry again."

"Don't say that. I would want you to be happy, just don't pick a selfish, young, beautiful, high-maintenance stepmom for my kids, okay?"

"Okay, good night love." It was dark but his tone meant he smiled. The silence lasted just a couple of minutes until my thoughts popped in and out of my mouth.

"When a person dies, you're gone. You'll just be gone, it won't matter to the person who died, just the people left behind, right?'

"I guess you're right, don't bring me back from heaven," he said adamantly and turned over.

"Good night honey, I love you."

"Forever and always?" I nudged him.

"Yes, forever and always," he said with a humph. He covered his head with a pillow, shutting down my nonsense.

I tried to close my eyes to sleep but my mind raced. I imagined what quirks of mine he would miss, like leaving cabinets open or hanging my bra everywhere. That led to trying to pick out the very best woman to take my place if I died before him. Just as he was drifting asleep, I blurted out my last wishes startling him. He jerked.

"Babe, I want to be cremated, so spread my ashes somewhere pretty that you and the kids can visit like the place from today or the lake or the botanical gardens would be nice. I want one of those lantern releases or a butterfly release. That would be nice."

"Babe, cremation? Why are we talking about this now, you aren't dying, you are very much alive and awake, let's go to sleep!"

So, I stopped talking but my mind did not shut off, instead, I laid there thinking up candidates for qualified women to marry my widowed husband...until my imagination gave out and I fell asleep.

My eyes opened at precisely 4:55 a.m. to my mother-in-law's front yard. There was a glow where the night was transitioning to a new day. A bird with the tiniest chirp made her front porch, its home. It greeted me and I returned with a smile. "Hi, little guy." I was happy I made it past 3 a.m. *Thank you, God, for another hour of sleep!* If I were seventy years old this would be a normal thing. I laughed. I slipped out of bed like a ninja, notebook, and Bible in hand crept to the sun porch. I just sat taking in the early sounds and smells of the dawn.

Speak to me, God. God, how did you prepare me for this? Holy Spirit, show me.

"How long have you been out here, want some coffee?" My mother-in-law in her robe summoned me inside to help make a full breakfast spread including palm-sized cinnamon rolls that were already rising.

Hard conversations.

I was laser-focused to lessen the financial burden of legal fees when we returned home. When I wasn't physically gathering all the unwanted things, I was mentally making lists of things to sell. Every pretty, eclectic, valuable, and sentimental item was brought out for the garage sale. It was a joint effort because we didn't have enough stuff, news of my fundraising spread, and soon neighbors, friends, and my mom were all dropping off things to be sold. These donations were selfless acts of love leaving me in awe of the Church. Saturday after Saturday I was listing and bargaining, sweeping the house for more things to sell. If we did not use it or play with it, if it collected dust, if it was worth more than I paid for it...it was sold. Some of the things represented memories like gifts, and those transactions were humbling. One in particular that pained me was an old clock.

"Mom, you aren't going to sell this clock, are you?" I slowly rubbed a towel across the distressed scrolled metal cross clock to dust it. The batteries had not been replaced, when it stopped ticking is a mystery, but it stopped at 12:36. I held it almost like a newborn, and a vision of Keith bringing it home flashed through my memory. I was making dinner when he came home carrying it in his hand. It was neglected but cherished. The first wedding anniversary present Keith gave me 14 years ago, surviving six moves. Now it will help to keep our family together.

"Yes, well if someone wants it for $10, then yes. But if not, it lives another week on the wall." I said with false confidence, my emotions turned off. It was a small sacrifice to pay for the attorney retainer. The kids were spared the financial and legal details, so I lied. I appreciate its contribution to the cause almost as much as when he surprised me with it as a bright-eyed bride. An unexpected gift from my new husband for our living room. He saw it from a department store window on his break and knew I would love it, and I did in fact love it. Selling this old cross clock or any of the other things left a small void in the house and in me. It was a humbling goodbye to the waffle maker, blender, bookshelf, keyboard, or any of the other items collected over the years that were sold for pennies on the dollar. My heart detached from the material things one by one. I mustered as much conviction in my voice as I could to hide the pain. I wanted to be strong for the kids and for Keith. We sold so much we joked about entering the mission field and moving to Africa. Ironically, I couldn't legally leave the country until the Grand Jury decision was over.

To keep our spirits up, we worshiped with the volume on high, I gathered more and more for the sale-stash and danced the blues away. The stash grew like loaves and fishes. It was piled in the garage as high as I could reach, and when that filled up, it spilled into a corner of the living room. Sometimes, we would just stare wondering where all the stuff came from? Where was it hiding, and how did it fit into 1200 sq. ft. before now?

I worshiped as I worked, both with the music and my incessant talks with God. It made a difference in my mood; my outlook was changing.

On one beautiful Saturday, an acquaintance from church sent me a message she wanted to lend a hand at my sale. Heather is a single mom with four kids of similar ages to mine. They shared the same Sunday school class, and she had heard about what we were going through. I didn't ask her how, but I am sure it was through a passed-around prayer request or the article in the paper. I was happy about the help. She arrived with a few things to contribute to the piles, a bubbly smile, and a new conversation as we waited for buyers.

My mom was with us this November Saturday. Her visits were a little more frequent since the accident, a good thing for an unfortunate reason. The kids love a visit from Nana; in their innocence, they didn't need a reason for the change. She comes bearing hugs, knick knacks, and her legendary loaves of fresh banana and apple bread to sell. That was all they needed to know, but Nana was a mom first. She was just as determined as her daughter to raise money for the highly recommended lawyer. What we didn't sell, we could eat.

It was slow that morning. We sat in folded chairs facing each other, talking about kids and whatnot and sampling the bread. We thought this sale might be a bust when the neighbor from just a few doors down wandered over and had his eye on an older model elliptical. I told my friend that gave it to us to sell, I could not accept such an expensive donation, but she insisted. He walked over with the biggest smile on his face like he had been on the hunt for one, "My wife will think I am a hero if I surprise her with it."

"I have a neighbor discount for you," I told him. Mr. Neighbor had a beard like Santa, and his cheerful demeanor completed the package. If Santa sported a flag and eagle tattoo. He always has a smile and patience for my rowdy kids and dogs. Despite the noise, he nor his wife ever complained. Plenty of times, our balls or frisbees have ended up in their yard, and they just toss it back over. I knew they were retired and liked to garden; that's all I knew of this couple. It warmed my heart how he wanted to gift his wife the elliptical.

"Okay," he grinned. "I tell you what, I need to go help one of my Veteran buddies out at the Legion, and when I get back, if it's here, I'll take it. I don't want you to hold it for me, though."

This is another moment where time stands still in my memory. No one but God understood. I knew the mention of "Veteran and the Legion" was significant, it triggered a reality and my heart began to beat out of my chest. Twisting and pounding like I was running uphill, and I knew in my heart God arranged this exact moment. I prayed the prayer, and I had hoped for it to be answered, but in God-type fashion, I would have never been able to think this one up. My mind went perfectly still, and I heard a thought like a pin drop; he knew David.

LEFT TURN, LIFE UNIMAGINED

I could have just nodded and smiled and kept it cordial, put a "sold" sign on the elliptical, and been done with it. God gave me a choice. I felt it in my gut. *I have provided a way; it is your choice.* I felt a stirring so strong in my spirit I swear I heard the Lord. I started to shake uncontrollably. I knew this may be my only chance, and so I reached out my hand and grabbed his. My eyes stung, and he did not understand my sudden emotion or why this stranger was reaching for his hand.

"Did you know David?" came out of my mouth before I could take it back. I looked straight into his eyes. I can't imagine how my voice quivered in that small voice with such a big question.

"I did," he tilted his head, trying to read me.

"It was me; it was my fault. And I am so very sorry for your loss!" the tears just streamed.

He pulled back his hand. Stiffened up and processed what I had just confessed. I braced for whatever would happen next but then, looking at my brokenness, he softened back to the jolly neighbor with a Santa smile. I saw a twinkle in his eyes.

"I would have never expected it to be you. We all thought it was a reckless driver or someone drunk."

I just shook my head no and let the tears fall.

"I just need you to know I stopped at the stop sign; I just didn't see him. I wish I did. If I could take it back, I would. I tried everything I could to save him. I am so very sorry, please forgive me!"

Seeing that I had no more strength to speak, my mom, also crying, came to my side and held me up. She put her arm around me at my waist to help me stand because my legs were weak from trembling.

He stood there quietly and was kind enough to share just a few details about the man I so desperately would like to know.

"Old Dave was a great guy, loved by everyone and friendly. He loved his kids, a family man, and loved Jesus. The man who sold him that bike is distraught, blames himself. He's having a real hard time with guilt. His wife says he's a mess. One of our Legion buddies sold him that Harley just a few hours before the crash. It's a shame. He had been at the Legion for dinner; everyone said you could see the excitement all over his face about that new bike. But no one knows why he was coming back up there. No one knows why he turned around. I know you barely know me but don't beat yourself up like this. I know Dave, and he wouldn't want this for you. I will talk to the other officers of the club and let them know it wasn't like what we thought."

His words were full of grace. This information also made me have more questions.

David, why did you turn around?

"Maybe someday I can come to talk with them. I will answer any questions the best I can."

He made a little gesture at his car so he could run that errand and assured me he would be back to buy the elliptical. I turned into my mother's shoulder and wept. Everything in me thanked the Lord for coordinating that conversation. The answer to my prayer was just a few steps away, and I never knew. This would not be the last time God showed me he was right there the whole time. Through every tear and every fear, he was with me. We made roughly $97 that day after splurging for a happy hour soda and slush for everyone.

Keith and the kids came spilling out of the truck just as we threw in the towel to pack up. Asher was quiet, and his cheeks were flushed. They had been at a church little league basketball game returning just in time for refreshments. Nana gave a round of hugs but thought it was time to head back to Dallas. She avoids driving at night now.

"Thanks for your help, mom!" I will take this little chunk of money from the attorney's office on Monday."

LEFT TURN, LIFE UNIMAGINED

"Wish we could have made more," her voice melancholy. I can only imagine how afraid she was for me on the inside. This is a parent's worst nightmare.

"No, Mom, this was great today. It was a good day; God answered my prayer, and that alone was worth it." We hugged goodbye.

Her hugs lingered just a little longer than before October 4th. Subtle differences of good changes.

The elephant in the room.

Asher has been acting strange since returning from the game. I wondered if he was disappointed in the score or how he played. My little competitor has a loud inner critic. His pouty face huffed and puffed, sighed, and grunted about the house.

I finally asked him, "Bubba, what's wrong?"

His sister cut eyes at him like daggers and said, "It's nothing. He is fine."

"Thank you, sis, but I asked Asher."

"Something happened at the game, but I am not supposed to talk about it."

"What do you mean you are not supposed to talk about it?"

"It's nothing, mom," Brooklynn said for him again.

Knowing something was up, and I was purposefully out of the loop made me upset. "I am your mother, Asher Keith, and we don't have secrets in this house."

With tears in his eyes, he said, "A kid after the game asked me if you were going to go to jail. I told him to shut up, but are you?"

"Asher, I told you don't ask her that!" Brooklynn was furious with him.

The question, I'll admit, was something I wasn't prepared for. The rug had been pulled out from under me and I landed on my back. This was the elephant in the room. We should name this elephant "Future" because it's always there in the room wherever I go. We didn't know how to explain the things that might happen or might not happen. I was just so happy from God answering a prayer with the neighbor, I was more than happy, I was elated. That made the fall from this question a harder blow. How do I even respond to that?

From the stern look on Keith's face, it appeared he too had told Asher everything would be fine, that this was not something he needed to worry about. But my ten-year-old was worried, and he wasn't letting it go. "I told you; Mommy is not going to jail. It was an accident. End of discussion." Keith really would not even speak about the possibility.

Connor, the oldest, is naturally strong-willed and opinionated but has been silent on the matter. Something from what Keith said caught his teenage attention to engage the conversation and away from the TV.

"Why would you go to jail? That's dumb! It wasn't your fault!" He shouted in my direction.

"Connor, it was my fault." I tried to explain.

"No, he hit you, Mom, it wasn't your fault. It's stupid Asher, why would you think that? They can't just put innocent people in jail. Mom is innocent, it was just an accident!"

"Connor, he had the right of way. My lawyer doesn't think it will happen, but it is...." He stood up from the couch in protest and again with an adamant voice, "It wasn't your fault, mom. It was a horrible freak accident! This is dumb."

There was no reasoning with him; he only escalated. This was the frustration talking; his shell had cracked wide open, and out came anger. "It wasn't your fault, mom!" This was the first time he showed us what he had felt about the situation. He was angry, and he didn't understand what to do with those big feelings. I watched my son struggle to release tears, he shook his fist and stomped up the stairs to his bedroom. This was the first time he let us into what he was internalizing. He had every right to express it in his way. I did what I knew I needed, I just listened.

I tried to remain positive, but who was I kidding? The fear was there like something tugging on my shoulder, trying to win my attention. Tap-tap-tap, excuse me, you can't think about the future because you don't know if you have one. The Grand Jury was coming. I couldn't just be happy and pretend that away. One painful day at a time because His mercies are new every day. Looking at the big picture was impossible; I spent the energy getting from moment to moment and trying to find the good. Each day, God faithfully provided some small moment of laughter, something that made me smile, and the icing on the cake was gratitude, there was always something to be grateful for. Today I am grateful for an answered prayer and that Connor finally opened up. You can't heal what we don't acknowledge.

Something unexpected.

Coming out of hermit-life feels like when you stand up after sitting too long. It's like I've forgotten how to carry on a normal conversation. I'm making an effort; my therapist suggested initiating a routine. I should come with the warning label. *May start to cry for no reason. May overshare about all things considered TMI. Will bring up strange details about accidents that are heavy and unrelatable.*

Last Sunday after service, I cracked a distasteful joke with the youth minister's wife. Bless her heart, she is bright-eyed, rainbows and roses young. They don't have children yet. Unjaded by life which I won't hold against her. "It's crazy, right? Orange is not the new black; I can't wear bright orange; it's not my color." "I don't want to be anyone else's wife!" I could have stopped with inappropriate jokes about my situation, but I continued. I said it jokingly until my eyes watered, and she knew this was me trying to make light of a dire situation. Life has a way of presenting moments where all you can do is laugh or cry. "We've sold everything we can, perfect timing to join the mission field, right? But I'm not allowed to leave the country. Ba-dum-bum-ching! Can you believe that?" I laughed through my tears. My eyes revealed the truth, this wasn't funny, none of it was. Thankfully she saw through it, this facade of me trying to be sociable.

"We are praying as hard as we can," she responded. The air between us turned somber, and then she hugged me. Which was perfect because I needed someone to hold the space as uncomfortable as it was for both of us.

The evening continued, and by 6 o'clock, I was spent emotionally, on the verge of exploding on someone or spending the rest of the night curled up in my bed. But something unexpected happened. After fifteen years of marriage, Keith looked at my fragile weary soul, offered me his hand, and said, "Come on, let's get some air, let's go for a walk together." I put my hand in his, and he helped me off the couch. Immediately the kids followed suit, thinking it was a family affair.

"No, just me and mommy are going for a walk," he said firmly. The kids were not thrilled with this idea. "Lock the door behind us. You have our phone; we will just be around the block."

What if we get run over? Is this safe? Does he want to talk about me going to jail? Despite all my questions in my head, I just put a sweatshirt on with my pajamas, and we walked the neighborhood hand in hand. I turned my flashlight on my phone to help alert people that drove past us. It's funny because I know it did nothing to penetrate the dark, a motorcycle headlight was missed, this phone light will do nothing to protect us. So, I asked God for protection. *Let your angels go before us, Lord. Surround us with a hedge of protection.*

"Can you think of anything else we can sell?" I asked him to break the silence.

"Sell whatever we need to; all we need is each other and a cardboard box." He flashed a smile and kissed the back of my hand that fit so perfectly in his. He gives me the feeling that people write about in romance novels. *God, I don't deserve this man!*

"Cardboard box, it's a big, big box with lots and lots of rooms," clapping to the beat of an old song from our youth, "Come and go with me to my cardboard box."

"You're silly," I think this glimpse of the old me made him emotional, he didn't show it, but I felt it.

The sky was clear, and a good amount of stars were out. It was chilly enough that we could see our breath, but it was refreshing. For most of the walk, we did quietly, which was just what my spirit needed. This was a good quiet, he had recognized I was overstimulated. Over the years our hands have formed to one another. I noticed that when a car approached, he held me tighter.

"We need to do this more often and take time for just the two of us without the kids even if it's just going for a walk or a breakfast date."

"I would like that."

My love for him grew; the more love grew, the more I had to resist the sadness that this could change after the Grand Jury decision. At this moment, he gave me the gift of unconditional love. And because I love him so much, how could I ask him to wait for me while I serve a prison sentence? Cliche or not, I love him more now than when we said I do. The miracle at this moment was that Keith had no idea of knowing how significant this walk was. When I was eleven or twelve years old, my parents went through a rough patch in their marriage. They were approaching their 15th wedding anniversary; as a nosey first-born, I discovered that their "dates" were appointments to marriage counseling. I remember them taking a walk, just the two of them. At first, my little sister and I were offended, but when we saw them return talking and laughing from their 20-minute escape, the hurt feelings faded.

This walk with Keith was a gift, something I knew I would always treasure, and it couldn't be hung on a wall or sold in a yard sale. Forever in my heart.

The walk gave me something to journal about when insomnia hit. I used the sleepless night to do heart-work in the bottom of my closet. Seeking hope in the Word and getting lost in journaling to God, to David and to my future self. Trying to find me, the real me. The me that felt comfortable in her skin, the one who smiled and laughed and believed in a good God and loving Savior. She was in there, there were glimpses of Jenna Lynn like celebrity sightings, but without the celebrity part. I just get excited to see the old me in any form. I wanted the song in me to return. The glass half-full type girl. I reflected and processed, and most of all, I prayed through the dark hours of the night, finding my true me would mean seeking the Lord with my whole heart first.

11-13-2016

Beautiful moon, brilliant moon.
Watchful keeper guarding the night.
Mystical, enchanting, restful, and still
You are unchanging, trusted light.
Beautiful moon, glowing moon.
Why can I not sleep?
It's in the night fear creeps, slaying me.
The glory of your light is all I see as I weep.
Beautiful moon, stunning moon
How many tears have you watched me shed?
The only comfort is that soon there will be a new day.
Established, like the Psalms I pray from bed.

Crumble or crack, panic attack.

Officer Kurt's calls were always professional and kind. I knew it was routine for him. I cannot imagine juggling cases of people like me. Phone calls to the driver, calls to the victim's family; it was a lot. For this call, I stepped outside to better hear him, but it was chilly, so I sat in my old car. My Ford had remained stationary, parked in the same spot from that night. I hate this car. Some people love their car, give them pet names and I was on the opposite spectrum. I wished I could beat this car with a bat and set it on fire. It's the only time in my life I could imagine being violent. I hate this car, it hurt David.

"Bring $7 cash with you unless you prefer a check; you won't be able to use your debit card. You'll want to pull around back and park across from the jail. Follow the signs. Gayle or Rose will be there to help you." Officer Kurt was always to the point.

The much-anticipated crash report was complete, and it was ready for pickup, but I wasn't sure I was ready. I had built this report up in my mind that it would hold all of the answers. The investigation findings were in a legal-sized folder waiting for the Grand Jury to deliberate over. This report is a critical component of how the jury will perceive my actions from that night. I envisioned the document room; this stack of papers would make a heavy thump before me; it would be intimidating to read through. I would gather them from the registrar, and they would look me over as the woman who killed David. I wondered if I would understand the legal words in a report like this. My anxiety dangled a carrot before my imagination, and away they went.

"Yes, sir, thank you." finding my words was a struggle; my emotions swept over me like a tidal wave. In a month, it feels like a long time away and an incredibly short amount of time too.

JEN EIKENHORST

The Grand Jury will meet in a small courtroom in the old limestone courthouse, sit around an oval wood table, and listen to facts that determine futures. Mine is one of them. The news of a timeframe was welcome; my mental limbo to a degree now had a checkpoint; the not-knowing felt as if it would go on forever. It gave me a deadline to prepare to get some things in order. I almost dropped the phone from shaking. I had to wait it out in the car and let the emotions have their way with me before returning inside. It is finished. It's in God's hands now; it always was.

Dear God, give me strength.

I put on my big girl panties to retrieve my crash report. Again, this feeling of responsibility of owning up came over me. I felt I should be the one to do it; I would walk into the Sheriff's office and face the music. On my drive to the office, I hoped there would be answers or at least theories of why and how I didn't see him. My hands gripped the steering wheel in the car, and I talked to myself the whole drive over. I made up my mind that if this report did not have all the answers, as I had hoped, I must have a brain tumor. If Officer Kurt could find no other logical explanation in all his wisdom and experience, my brain would be to blame. "It's my peripherals," I thought to myself. "A brain tumor or malfunction of my eyes." The only reasons why I didn't see him.

However, in God's perfect timing or a cruel plot of the enemy, my side views proved to be working today. A yellow road sign suddenly caught my attention. It was a motorcycle symbol, and it read, "*Share the Road.*" I've seen this slogan countless times before, but, on this day, it created an inner earthquake on a two-lane road towards the Sheriff's office.

My chest became so tight I had to arch my back and strain to catch each breath. My thoughts were a mess as I repeatedly said out loud, "Share the road, share the road, Jenna, share the road!" Did someone put that sign there just for me? I would share the road; I always share the road! I would have shared the road with him. God, help me breathe. Why can't I breathe? A burning crawled across my chest and up my throat. Maybe I should pull over, I thought. I'm almost there, I rebutted to myself. My hands began to tingle. I gripped the wheel so tight the color left them. I wanted to throw up. I wanted to scream, "I just didn't see him!" "Share the road, Jenna." I was so filled with rage, my eyes stung, my nose burned, I wanted to fight the person who made that sign. I thought about running away, driving away.

I was here. Officer Kurt referred to this area as the Law Enforcement complex, but it resembled a compound next to the county jail. I followed the signs directing to the back, and when I parked, I thanked God, I made it. I sat for a second, waiting to die; this was it. Surely the stabbing pain of a heart attack would come, but it didn't. My pounding relaxed to a thump, to pitter-patter, to a dull ache.

God, give me courage.

I walked into the Sheriff's office with a splotchy red face as if I biked my way here and the wind had burned my cheeks. I wondered if this is where the processing might happen? Is this where Keith will come to bail me out? I was so very nervous and weighted but I wanted to see the report. Maybe something would make sense. I passed a man walking out shaking his head at a white document rolled up in his fist. What if it was David's brother? Officer Kurt had mentioned a brother that had been following the investigation closely. Was he there for the same report? I approached the registrar's window and there was a little sign that hung from the ceiling, *Crash Reports Here*. I waited patiently for the woman to address me.

"Yes ma'am, how can I help you?" a gentle voice asked from behind plexiglass. She had perfectly wavy silver hair, not a single strand out of place and dainty shoulders covered by a crocheted shawl. Her nails matched her lipstick and I thought of my grandmother. The name tag read, Gayle.

My voice began to shake. "Hi, I am here to get a copy of a crash report, my name is Jenna Anderson." I was already swallowing back tears, ashamed of my own name.

"Oh, sweetie here I had it ready for you. Kurt said you would be on your way." She passed the packet of papers through the glass opening. My hand shook to grab it, "Thank you." I could barely speak. The tears had their way once again.

"Is it $7 for the copy?" I started to slide the crumpled money under the window, and she waved it away.

"You have been through enough," she said. She knew who I was, my name, and what I had done. I was known in the Sheriff's office, and it was met with compassion.

"Thank you," I whispered and turned, feeling overwhelmed by her kindness. I didn't know how to receive grace. I thought I might crumble to the cold black and white tile floor.

I made it back to the car clutching the manilla envelope and had to let this wave of emotions roll out like the tide. "Calm down," I told myself. "You can barely see through your tears." This little talk alone in the car caused me to laugh out loud, I snorted. I tried to look at the report, but I couldn't see through the pooling of my tears. "It's like opening my eyes under freaking water." Laughter erupted again, "This is ridiculous. I'm delirious. I've lost my mind."

Last week we went to a friend's church to see their daughter be baptized, and I lied about my name. Who does that? What if they recognized it from the paper? What if they knew him, so I lied on the church childcare registry for Hazel. I wrote down that my name was Jennifer Henderson on the parent info card and reversed my cell phone numbers. What has happened to me?

Thinking back about this lie in the church made me cringe but out came more outbursts of laughter. "Just breathe." I had to catch my breath from laughing. I lied in church about my name. I can imagine if someone did need me and they asked Hazel, "Isn't this your mommy's name?" She would have let them know, "Nope, she lied." Shrugged her shoulders and went on playing.

It took courage to get here, to this point in the Law Enforcement Complex parking lot. I looked at the envelope, knowing there was nothing it could hold that was scarier than the reality of October 4th. I noticed the envelope was thin, really thin. I slipped open the brass prongs and pulled out a three-page report stapled together. Half of it was just logistics of make, model, and specifics of my own personal information. There was a simple box diagram showing a complex situation. My left-hand turn was oversimplified. Arrows depicted the motion of the vehicles. The motorcycle was a stock image graphic approaching my car marked by a big box and a red X. The right of way was labeled and a key to explain all the symbols.

"This isn't what it was like!" I shouted. "Where is the freaking hill? Or the tree blocking my vision? Where is the darkness?" This explains NOTHING!

This was the equivalent of a stick figure drawing of a crash scene. Who the hell made this? Hazel could have done a better job. Leaving tons of questions to an untrained perspective. There was no obstructed view from hanging tree limbs. There wasn't any explanation of divots in the road or hill elevation, or even where I sat at the stop sign back four feet behind where the actual road began. I felt as if the computer sketch did not do the story justice. Nothing would justify that night; I was hoping that maybe Officer Kurt had figured everything out so that I would know why. But no such luck, and now I was heated. *If this is what will be presented to the jury, it's over. I would convict myself. It will take a miracle. Lord, it would be a miracle to see this explanation and for the hearts of the jurors to see beyond the lines.*

JEN EIKENHORST

I still remember when my dad took me to a big open mall parking lot in Dallas to learn how to drive. It was early on a Sunday morning, so he knew the Park's Mall would be deserted.

He said, "Put your hands at 10 and 2 like this, and when we get to the stop sign, you always count to three. Look left, look right, and look left again." I remember coming up to a crossing section as we drove around the abandoned mall, and even though no one was there, he wanted me to pretend.

"You see this when you come up to an intersection you are always aware of everything around you. Do not just fixate on any one thing, but your eyes should be moving at all times. And never assume anyone sees you or sees that stop sign. Assume that they don't and be ready if they run it." I gripped that wheel so tightly, and I held on to every word he said. My dad was the best teacher. Twenty years of defensive driving, gone. It didn't matter anymore. But this memory is so tangible I can see it in my mind's eye. Almost sixteen sitting in my dad's Corolla full of happy, nervous energy and soaking in all the wisdom of how to be a safe responsible driver.

Breaking point.

It was the day of the annual blanket drive, and I was forced to make an unplanned trip up to the school. The kids left their material to make blankets sitting on the kitchen counter. I didn't want them to be the only kids without something to contribute. It taunted me. I had to go in there. I had to face people that have hurt my husband. I found myself brainstorming about other ways to deliver the fabric without seeing anyone.

Drive up and honk, throw the bag and leave. Drop the bag at the school door; someone would see it. Wait for the postman; maybe he would take it in. I even reasoned, what is one or two fewer blankets? They might not need it anyway. In the end, I decided this was my one hard thing for the day. This might actually count for five because of the pain this school has caused my family. Jenna, put those big girl undies on and go, I thought to myself. This was now a mantra, grab your trusted panties that give you the audacity you need to face whatever curve ball is coming. Funny, I visualize courage from underwear and not something more sensational like a cape or a mask. Those panties must have bunched up in a wad because I was in a mood. I brushed my hair for this, made sure I had a clean shirt on for this, graced my eyelashes with some mascara for this, and out I went to rescue the blanket drive.

I made a mad dash to the office with a note taped to the Walmart sack to explain who, where, and what the fabric was for, hoping I wouldn't need to talk.

As I was leaving, Missy held the door to come in behind me. She tilted her head slightly to the right, and with a sweet, innocent southern voice, she said, "Jenna, haven't seen you in a while, stranger; how are y'all doing?"

Did she want to know, or was she just playing nice? If she did, she wasn't prepared for my reply. This woman was in the unofficial gossip committee. Maybe it was the head tilt that got me or her flawless hair and makeup that rubbed me the wrong way.

"Missy, how the hell do you think we are doing? Yep, I said hell, hell hell hell hell hell! It sucks, Missy! It's the hardest thing I've ever lived through and maybe the hardest thing I ever will. I am not sure anyone on the school board, including your husband, has an ounce of integrity, yet we keep smiling. We keep showing up day by freaking day. I'm either headed to a nut house or prison, so there you go. That's how we are doing, and you can tell the gossip committee I don't care!"

My outburst rendered her speechless. Her jaw dropped wide open in shock, and I coldly strutted on by. I was shaking like a kernel in a greased skillet, but I shed zero tears. My teeth were clenched, I could have fought somebody with the rush of letting her have it.

This teapot cracked under the pressure and Missy just happened to be the recipient. My heart did flip-flops all the way back home.

Regret and remorse followed me. I was disappointed with our Christian leadership at our small private school but of all the people, Missy was the least deserving of my anger. The Holy Spirit reminded me of all the small moments I had with her, she was not anywhere near gossip circles. She wouldn't touch them with a ten-foot pole. That was the anger talking, that was the comparison monster in my ear. Missy represented the mom I wish I was for my kids. She seemed to have it all together, she didn't forget the material for the blanket drive. I can't hold that against her, everyone's you-know-what stinks. We have different stinks, but we each have it.

Later that night I tried to call her. I left a voicemail when she denied my call and I apologized for my tirade. I asked her to forgive me. The book of Matthew 15:18 says, "Out of the mouth comes from the heart." My heart was as heavy as it was dark, and the anger was shameful. Whether what I said felt true or not it was uncalled for and it made me feel worse, not better. This must be what Dr. Knox meant by "prickly" or sensitive and the unexpected anger that might flare occasionally. People avoided me like the plague after that, if I wasn't a topic of interest before my tantrum, I certainly made the circuit now.

Sermon illustrations.

Keith and I decided it was time to put forth an effort to return to church more regularly. That following Sunday in service, the associate pastor was doing a three-part series about the life and death of Jesus. A little unorthodox leading into the Christmas season, typically, we partake in the story of a pregnant virgin and a miracle birth.

But as soon as he shared about his father's failing health, the inspiration behind the sermon message was apparent. Death was imminent, a matter of waiting. Was there hope in death? "But God is still working in the waiting," a strong point he made during the arch of the sermon. He had a ticket on standby to fly home. His raw perspective of feelings about death and anticipating grief stirred me.

Waiting for death, I immediately thought of David's children in their waiting. Emotions were building. I tried with everything to listen and not make this sermon about me. Recovering from trauma has a self-centered lens; for me, almost anything can trigger my wounded soul.

Pastor Lonnie has prayed with many on their deathbeds or with their loved ones saying goodbye. Over twenty years in ministry, he has plenty of experience. Despite all the opportunities to serve alongside the grieving, admittedly dealing with it personally was different.

Transparency led the way to vulnerability, and we were all witness to its beauty; his voice cracked, then an intense pause that spoke in its silence. He choked back tears, but they managed to escape. I gave way to my own tears.

I did that, I told myself when I took him away from his children. I made those innocent kids feel like Brother Lonnie feels right now. I continued to struggle and squirm when Lonnie used a question from the pastorate wheelhouse, which was a dagger to my heart. "If you left this service today and had an accident on your way home. What if today you met your maker, would you know where your eternity lies?"

I couldn't hold it in. I was undone. I could not control the heaving and sobbing as I scooted past attentive patrons invested in every word of the emotional sermon. I climbed over what felt like endless knees and made my way to the aisle to exit. I needed to escape making a whole scene as I did so. I wanted out of that sanctuary, but I would not go discreetly as I was inconsolable.

David, did you know the Lord? I need to know. Oh God, what if he didn't because he went before his time? I need a sign. He was 300 feet from safety Lord, 300 freaking feet! Just a minute's drive to safety. Lord, why didn't you tell him to turn around? Did he tell you not to buy that bike, David? Why not wear a helmet? Would your helmet have saved you? Oh God, I hate this! Why is this real?

Up until now, I was in the ring, fighting every day for life. This round was a total KO. I wasn't sure I had the backbone to crawl out of the women's bathroom stall. I sent Keith a text to meet me in the car. Our Associate Pastor did not write that sermon for me. I wasn't the sermon illustration, but I very well could be, or a punch line of a joke. But this was not meant to convict me. It was simply the truth. Raw and honest truth. Nice-guy David met his maker just hours after buying that Harley and just a short distance from his destination to safety. That line about the frailty of life is not just a "tactic" to draw emotion from the congregation. It is real. *Do you know where your eternity lies? David, did you know?*

One of the older kids asked if we could go to lunch after church. Keith and I knew it wasn't financially possible. Friday, we had fist-bumped to celebrate $.76 left in our account with more money coming in at midnight Monday morning. We had to make do with what was left in the pantry.

"Guys I thought it would be fun if we had pancakes for lunch." I looked to the backseats to their hungry faces.

"Okay," they cheered. I had not made pancakes since before the accident.

Making pancakes for six people on a griddle took a second to find the rhythm. Some of the pancakes were a little toasty, some misshapen and a few flips landed off the griddle altogether, but it worked. "Man down," I would shout, contributing to the family felt good. It was a victory. The kids declared their love for my pancakes and how much they "missed" them. It was more than a cheap and easy meal but the return of a family tradition.

We didn't talk about the sermon or my public meltdown. I decided to shake this one off and move on. Instead, favorite toppings for pancakes and what variations might be fun made for better conversation. We made bets over who would win a pancake eating contest and who could eat one in a single bite. I sat near Asher, and he seemed to need me a little more than the other three children on this day. He craved my attention, and he did so by sharing all he knew about rocks and minerals. He wanted me to know all the facts too, spouting them off in one continuous rock and mineral trivia card deck. I let him share until his heart's content.

"Mom, did you know that graphite and a diamond are made up of the same carbon?" Asher proudly began to tell us the differences between something so soft that goes in a pencil and then the same material, bright and valuable like a diamond.

"Do you know what makes them different and why a diamond is so strong?"

Some of us knew the answers to his question and burned to steal the limelight, but we gave a quick side-eye to Connor to let his little brother tell us.

"Asher, go ahead, tell us?"

"It's the heat and pressure. The graphite is brittle because it has not been under the same heat as a diamond. The structure is more complex and therefore stronger." As he gave us all the specifics, I just nodded and smiled at our little rock enthusiast. I was reminded of that verse where God uses fire to refine us. To get out all the impurities. We were certainly walking through the fire, but I can't imagine coming out of this like shiny gold or beautiful and strong like a diamond. Was God talking to me through my son because that was an excellent sermon illustration if I ever heard one!

I feel like I have taken a few steps backward in healing. Dr. Knox said it is common to make progress and pull back, cha-cha forward, and then fall back. Healing has no timeline and there is a natural ebb and flow, a constant adjusting to rhythms. At the forefront of every thought was the approaching Grand Jury. Would I be able to face going to prison? I was taking it minute by minute and I didn't see life past next month when jurors would hear the facts of my case and decide my burden of guilt.

I have always been a little naive, believing the good in people and that justice always wins. Now that I have to put my faith where my mouth is, it wasn't that easy. The declaration from a judge or jury would not change what I felt, which was tremendous guilt. *Was I a killer? Was David my victim?*

∴

We were in the fire, there was no doubt to anyone living life within our proximity that we were in the furnace. As much as I did not want to be in the fish bowl on display, I was watching too, looking for how God would work things out. 1 Peter 1:7, These have come so that the proven genuineness of your faith—of greater worth than gold, which perishes even though refined by fire—may result in praise, glory, and honor when Jesus Christ is revealed. As much as our faith was being birthed it was simultaneously being restored. Every impurity revealed, every false hope exposed, fully and completely dependent on the Lord.

Series of firsts.

It was almost Thanksgiving, and we were headed back to East Texas celebrating early with my in-laws outside of Tyler. In just a few weeks there will be a wedding in our family for New Year's Eve. It pained me to think maybe I wouldn't be there. What if things didn't work out as we thought with the Grand Jury?

The task of the relish tray was bestowed on me. This felt manageable. Cans of olives black and green, variety of pickles to fancy the taste buds of sweet, savory, sour, and spicy. Baby corn for fun and pickled carrots, sliced radishes and the star, deviled eggs. I grabbed my favorite yellow platter that thankfully still had not sold from the garage sale pile. It's one of the only things I had left from my wedding shower. I took pleasure in arranging the tray.

In my family, I caught what we call the "giggles" while making the deviled eggs. I don't know if the lack of sleep contributed or I had certifiably lost it upstairs, but I was thoroughly overcome with joy. I didn't realize I was still capable of experiencing joy. It dawned on me that the little boiled eggs resembled a toilet bowl. Laughter erupted from the pit that had been buried by sorrow. It wasn't pretty. I laughed so hard it caused a disturbance.

One by one, they came to the kitchen to check on me. I laughed until tears rolled down my cheeks. I could barely get out words. I banged my hand on the counter laughing so hard I couldn't breathe. I was so tickled; I crossed my legs at the knees to not pee my pants.

"Look at the eggs, don't you see? It's like a toilet bowl filled with poop. See the swirl!"

"Mom, that's so gross!" Brooklynn was not amused at first. "I know! That's why it's so funny," I squealed. "What do you mean, honey, what is poop?" Keith was puzzled but laughing at me in this state of complete hysteria. "These eggs," I snorted. I squeezed the sandwich bag of yolk filling, and there was a bubble, it splats everywhere. I roared with contagious laughter. I've made deviled eggs dozens of times, and never did I see the swirl of yolk, mayonnaise, and mustard the same way. "Fitting, I would bring the toilet bowls filled with poop for Thanksgiving," I stammered. "Jenna brings the poop!" Everyone stood laughing with me or at me, but mainly they were stunned at this immense joy. It was good medicine, the laughter, and we all needed this moment. That time mom laughed so hard she cried because deviled eggs look like toilet bowls filled with poop. Never again would I look at deviled eggs the same.

We arrived with our relish tray, and tiny porcelain bowls only 30 minutes later than planned. In years past, I would have been frazzled, biting heads, and complaining that we were inconveniencing other people. Not now, that was pre-accident mom. Now my anxiety is all tied up on getting there safely with appetizers in tow.

The cousins were running around, capturing selfies. Someone is always laughing, and someone else is always trying to sneak a nibble. Now that some of our nieces are married, we spill out into every room of this big house.

Holidays represent "firsts," the first event without someone. Thanksgiving would be a first without him for David's family. Grief can rob the spirit of the holidays. The excitement of seeing family and smelling Mom's homemade pumpkin bread was not the same. Fall wreaths and mini pumpkins are displayed in the center of the table. A thoughtful tablescape made with love, but I could not appreciate it. No matter how hard I tried to get in the spirit of thankfulness, I felt empty.

After we said grace, I noticed my brother-in-law got up to grab something. The empty chair was a reminder. I zoned in on his empty chair. It was an out-of-body experience floating around the room, watching everyone enjoying their meal. My heaping plate of comfort food waited for my spirit to return. This was a dreaded "first" for his family, and I shared in it somehow. I don't know why I included myself in the grief of their "first holiday without Dad," but I did.

Family is a blessing, I thought. We don't know how good we have it for us all to be together like this, passing bowls of mashed potatoes and baskets of rolls, catching up with life events. The Dallas Cowboys game played in the background; a touch down paused the rumble of voices, and cheers erupted. They didn't have this, so I felt I shouldn't either. My mind could not help but go there. Somewhere because of me, the chair would remain empty.

My cell phone rang, and Strawn Office flashed across the screen. Startled by the surprise call, I quickly excused myself from around the firepit. I found privacy on the floor of the laundry room.

"Yes, sir," I answered.

"Jenna, I wanted you to know that the Trooper in charge of your case has been called to the border. If he isn't back, we will need to postpone your hearing."

"Okay, what do I need to do?" I asked.

"We need to have you come by the office soon to prep you as if things will go as expected for December 14th. Your case needs to be heard before December closes out. Odds of indictment go up in January with a new jury so let's just hope that Mr. Kurt can complete his tour and get back."

"Okay, we will ask our prayer warriors to add that specifically."

When we hung up, I rested against the washing machine for a solid five minutes, just thinking about the timing of Officer Kurt's border patrol rotation. There's no one I can call to be like, " Hey, can someone switch with Kurt? He is needed back in Lake Hills, so a woman named Jenna lowers her chances of going to prison." The crisis at the border was pretty serious, and who am I? It is what it is, this is out of my control, and in God's hands, it always has been.

I rejoined the circle of people making smores and sharing stories. The chatter grew quiet with my return. I sat and buried my hands into the cuffs of my sweater and cried. Because I knew they wanted to know. The tears are a constant drip of a leaky faucet. I wiped them away one by one with my sleeve.

"That was my attorney, the Trooper will be getting in touch with me about my hearing, and he said it is crucial that this Grand Jury hears my case. New jurors in January are typically nervous and are more likely to indict everyone until they are comfortable with their understanding of the laws. We just have to pray that my case makes the docket in December before being dismissed for Christmas. The Trooper in charge of my case is being summoned to the border. We don't know for how long exactly."

I glanced around at the faces that have known me since I was a senior in high school, and they didn't know how to respond. This is my world now, not theirs. I can't imagine hearing news like this if I were them. My sweet sister-in-law spoke up first and put her arms around me, "We are going to believe for that, Jenna. The right people will see this for what it is, an accident."

The support from my extended family was invaluable. Still, I knew what I was facing could change everything in a heartbeat. They would need to be there for Keith and the kids, and I would completely understand if our marriage fell apart.

The trial comes with a five-figure price tag-almost a year of my teacher's salary, and we don't have that kind of money. We've sold everything except bare necessities just to hire Mr. Strawn.

Besides, garage sales will not profit the money we would need for a trial. We would need a miracle. Pleading guilty would mean the loss of my teaching license. The fate of my life with a few words and a clank of a gavel. I could take a plea bargain to save money and heartache on the family. I would face a range of scenarios from ankle monitors to low-security camps, eighteen months to three years in prison. Every possible outcome came with a cost. We were in a pressure cooker. Only coal could come from this kind of pressure or a mental breakdown, or worse, a divorce. All I could do, we could do, was put one foot in front of the other, depending on God to sustain us.

•••

Philippians 4:6-7, Do not be anxious about anything, but in everything by prayer and supplication with thanksgiving let your requests be made known to God. And the peace of God, which surpasses all understanding, will guard your hearts and your minds in Christ Jesus. Saying we will not be anxious is very different from what our biological reflexes will put in motion. The body does its thing. Jesus holds your hand in those times we have no control.

Feeling sentimental.

The physical month had changed from November to December, and it felt like time was slipping away. The Christian scripture wall calendar was stuck in October. We were all "stuck," and I suddenly felt overly sentimental about everything. Money was stretched even tighter, tensions were higher, and the elephant in every room behind every turn was the approaching Grand Jury hearing. I wanted December 14th to come fast, yet I was terrified of how quickly time would pass without wishing for it.

Two months flew by, and I felt every minute of every hour pass. Eight Tuesdays behind me, adapting to a new normal as an accidental killer. It's a weird concept, all of it, time, somehow it felt as if it were an enemy. The passing weeks did not lighten the burden of the accident. People stopped asking questions and began putting the memory of the tragedy behind them, but I could not. As much as I wished I could leave it in October and move forward, I had this nagging feeling it was still yesterday that everything changed.

I had an appointment with the psychiatrist, a female doctor that Dr. Brad had suggested. Took weeks to get in. She was friendly and systematic; unlike Dr. Knox, her office felt professionally decorated and not cozy. I missed his soft smile and occasional chuckles. I missed the frumpy pillows that always landed in my lap to hold while I talked. However, we did have a productive discussion about techniques like grounding, breathing, and meditation to help with my anxiety. She and Keith encouraged me to do more normal things, so I promised to make an effort to venture out.

If I stay home, I'm safe from people asking questions they don't want to know the answer to. I don't embarrass my family with my appearance or my situation. If I look normal, I'm judged for moving on. I will never move on, ever. I felt I could not look happy. What kind of person looks happy when they have hurt someone else and are facing something so serious? I can't look too sad because then people will worry about me and if I am going to hurt myself. Some of this was my anxiety talking, overthinking everything, but some of it was valid. Regardless, I promised to try. Eased back with a church service, made an appearance at a basketball game, and even went to the grocery store.

I decided to explore the not-as-new grocery store, and this time I smiled at people; the last time I was here, it was for the memorial for David. I took the time to get every free sample. I left, and nothing terrible happened. No one pointed at me and gawked or whispered as I passed by. I was a regular mom, shopping. When I arrived home, I was greeted by a package. My sister and brother-in-law sent us a smoked turkey. Every year they send us one, every year they think of us and every time, the timing is perfect. Even though I could not imagine how this would all work out, I believed it would be okay.

I had the boys bring in the groceries, and as I stood watching them, I couldn't help but wonder where the time had gone. Their hands and muscles had grown because it only took one trip as they were determined to get all the bags in at once. Suddenly they looked so big. On a whim, I wanted to hold them. They had long outgrown my lap, but I realized my emotional distance from them lately. I wondered how I, as their mother, would affect them as men and choosing their future wives. Surviving my depression demanded energy and attention; the boys were left fending for themselves. "Just sit in my lap," I pleaded. "I want this memory. Come on, humor me."

"Mom, it's too late; we don't fit in your lap." Connor rolled his eyes in protest, and Asher blushed.

I patted my lap with a goofy grin. They eventually complied with my strange request anyway. I couldn't make up for lost time, but I am willing to not take time and family for granted any longer. Holding my sons infused my soul. One was now becoming a man-child as he is taller than me, his shoulders now broader, looking like Keith a little more every day, and the other not far behind him. There was different grief that twinged my heart that day and I wanted to hold them and imagine their smaller bodies that depended on their momma.

I washed the dishes and appreciated the energy it took to cook and clean after dinner. To the outside world I was contributing to the household, fulfilling a motherly duty. To my family they felt mom was returning. But I stood there hands deep in greasy sink water, I asked the Lord if my children would be okay. Do you remember Jenna when you realized your parents were messy and human and trying their best? Not particularly the exact moment Lord, but yes. They'll see that too, he said.

That night Hazel asked me to tuck her in and say prayers. I couldn't remember the last time I had partaken in the bedtime routine. Brooklynn was a champion of her little sister with fairytales, heroic classic tales and prayers. She did for Hazel what I did for her. I didn't want to miss any more opportunities. I leaned against the doorway of her room, and there she was on the bottom bunk waiting for me. Laying on her belly, feet kicking the air, her nose in the story she picked out, pretending to read it. Her face lit up when she saw me. I knelt, and she motioned for me to sit beside her. We prayed for her booboo on her knee and for good dreams. "Mommy, sing me that song, go to sleep, go to sleep."

"Okay." I smiled, my nose and eyes stung with emotion before a note was sung. Clearing my throat, I whisper-sang this little made-up lullaby. "Go to sleep, go to sleep, go to sleep, little Hazel. When you wake, in the morning, we will play. Go to sleep, go to sleep, close your eyes and dream." "La la la, la la hum hum hum hum la la la." A tear dripped from my nose to her cheek as I kissed her goodnight. I wiped it away.

"Momma, was that snot?"

"No, Hazel," I laughed.

"Did I make you cry?" She asked me.

"No, these are happy tears."

"Are you sad we don't have a table anymore? Where will we eat?"

"Yeah, I'm a little sad, but we'll picnic on the floor if we have to, but we'll be together just the same. Or God will give us a new one."

Earlier that day, I sold the last valuable item in our home, my heirloom dining table. Her question made me realize she was watching; she was processing the changes even at four years old. This was a grand table. Easily the nicest piece of furniture we ever owned, almost a work of art. It seated eight comfortably, hand-painted with antiquing around the edges. It was "solid," sturdy with intricate curved craftsmanship on the legs. The salesman convinced me it was from Italy and that pretty much sealed the deal. When we bought it with a tax return shortly after Asher was born the cost was justified by future hope in many meals to be shared around that table. I envisioned the family celebrations to come, the kids bringing home future boyfriends/girlfriends even spouses someday. But the table was needed in the present more, selling it would mean my attorney retainer was paid in full.

Within an hour of posting, Hand-painted Italian Craftsman Table-like new, a newly engaged woman messaged me that she had $400 cash in hand. Her fiancé had a truck, and they were eager to pick it up as soon as possible. Soon it was loaded, and they were beaming with excitement from their purchase.

"It's a good one, brought us lots of memories and I pray it blesses you both."

"It's perfect," she said, "thank you again." And they drove off to their future.

•••

Philippians 4:19 "And my God shall supply all your needs according to His riches in glory by Christ Jesus." My heart was happier for that young couple than my grieving heart. I held the memories close, and I let go of the future I hoped for detached from the table. God would provide a new table, or he would let a plastic and metal foldable table be just as beautiful as the Italian one.

Countdown to Grand Jury.

I woke up at about 3 a.m., startled. My eyes opened to find Keith sitting up, watching me sleep. I can't imagine it had been too long since I dozed off because I remember glancing at the alarm clock, and it read 1 a.m.

"Honey, are you okay?"

He said in a frightened voice, "I feel weird, my chest is tight, and I am sweating all over."

"I am freezing." He was shivering.

"Want me to get another blanket? Water?"

"My heart feels like it will beat out of my chest, listen." I sat up and leaned over, met with the rhythm of a strong heart that was growing weary.

"It does sound loud but nothing unusual." His forehead felt clammy but not feverish against my forearm.

"Want me to call someone or get you something?"

"Just sit with me." He reached for my hand.

"Of course."

Dear God,

Please, I am not strong enough. I need his heart to be okay. I am not strong enough without him. Our family can't take anything else. Take this from him, Lord, the panic, the burden as provider and protector. Give him supernatural peace. Comfort him. Please, God, I can't do this, don't ask me to do this. His heart is whole; he is safe and healthy. We will get through this in Jesus' name. Dear God, help us get through this. Amen.

We turned on the scripture app, and the narrator read the Psalms, our fingers laced tightly in the darkness. At 220lbs of mainly muscle, this man gives off heat. It startled me that he was noticeably cooler. We let the verses wash over us clinging to the promise of God's comfort. We watched the night sky brighten and eventually the sunrise. Enduring this test in our marriage has been like running a marathon. My runner was nearing the end of the race, and his body was folding. With God's grace, we will cross that finish line wobbling together. One more week until the jury hears my case. Hopefully, closure on this will allow us all to heal.

"It's a new day, look the sun is coming up," and with that, he laid his head on my chest and fell sound asleep.

Oh God, thank you for another day, please watch over us. Keep Keith safe, we need him.

I stepped up my game, praying over Keith, this man who loved me so well. The enemy picked a fight with the wrong wife. The lioness was back, ready to battle the spiritual warfare. I started secretly declaring healing over his body as he slept. I would touch his hands and pray for favor in all he does, career or otherwise. Lord, to bless his thoughts. I prayed over him from head to toe. Sleepless nights used to pray. My spirit was not ready to yield to these attacks. I would pray over Keith and quietly make my way to the kid's rooms and pray over them deep into the night. With so many things out of my control, this was within my power and my privilege.

I showed my face at church again. During worship, I sang my heart out. Between the lyrics of the songs, I cry out, "I'm sorry, David, I'm so sorry." Both Keith and I wept from the presence of the Holy Spirit. My eyes were wide open when I saw in my mind a vision. It was David's face, and he was smiling in what I believe with my whole heart he was in heaven. I felt God call to me deep inside my chest. He is at peace here with me. There is no unforgiveness here, no regret, no pain nor suffering. It's time to lay this down. Surender it. With that picture of David in heaven, I was overcome. In the back corner pew of Lake Hills Baptist Church, I realized David was at peace. He had forgiven me for pulling out in front of him the moment it happened, and he was welcomed home to Jesus. It was time to accept that grace. It was the first time I let the idea of forgiving what happened sit with me. Maybe self-forgiveness and trusting God's plan again were the next steps in this journey.

The next song in service sealed the deal that God was 100% speaking to me. The band moved into a song I had not heard in years. Years, more than a decade! It was the song I sang as a high school junior in front of the Young Life student-led meeting barely seventeen, and I was in charge that day. *Oh Lord, You're beautiful. Your face is all I seek, and when your eyes are on this child. Your grace abounds to me. His grace abounds to me.*

God is good. Whether a soul on this earth ever believed what I saw and what happened, it wouldn't matter. I know that I know I couldn't make this up or orchestrate that moment. Hope was ablaze inside me, and I would live my life telling people who feel helpless and hopeless that God is good.

With each passing day, I knew I was closer to having at least some idea of what my future would look like. I would say, "I trust the Lord completely," but did I trust Him? Innocent people go to prison, so is he still faithful with that outcome? I did a lot of soul searching in these last three months. It was time to have an uncomfortable conversation with just me and the Holy Spirit. Sitting in the stillness of the car, my car, the very car that caused this pain I was waiting on the Lord. *I heard the Lord pulling on my heart. He whispered again, "Do you trust me?" Trust me with the outcome you want? Trust me with what you can't imagine? Trust me to put down your fears, your doubts, and your expectations?*

"What do you want me to say, God? I love you; you know that I do! I don't know what to pray for anymore." I hit the steering wheel as I wrestled with what I knew that I knew I needed to admit. "You want me to say I love you even if I go to jail? Do you want that for me, Lord? Does that make it better, justice? I screamed out to the emptiness; my voice echoed back in the car. So, I asked myself,

"Jenna, do you trust the Lord with all of it?" My forehead rested on my hands that gripped the wheel, and I listened for an answer.

"Do I trust you, Lord?" Sigh. My voice cracked; if it is your will for me to go to prison, I surrender. I will serve you while I am there. But I don't want to do it, and I won't ever understand, but I trust you to help me and protect me. I love you, Lord, even if it means I go to jail or prison. Just please take care of them, my babies, and Keith."

The crisis has a way of transforming the mind and expanding what we can humanly withstand. It causes you to think differently, pivot, adapt, and with God's grace, persevere whether it's a wayward child, divorce, diagnosis, or significant loss you are facing. As soon as I released the worry of what if I go to prison, I felt like the weight of a thousand fears faded. I didn't know what I had been carrying in that box of emotions. It was out of my control, and frankly, I was wary of waiting. I felt like nothing could be worse than what we had already walked. Not knowing what will happen is torturous. Waiting is a living hell. Accepting what may come couldn't be any worse than the wake of the accident. Anything anyone said or thought of me was not worse than the thoughts I struggled to take captive about myself.

All I had left was worship, "I surrender all Lord." I was emptied of all the worry, all the pride, all the control, "I surrender it all, Lord." My voice squeaked. Singing was the only thing that made sense in the intimate presence of the Lord. A melody came over my spirit and flowed. I began to sway. Sitting in the driveway, a heart song took flight into the space of my old Ford that caused so much devastation. I heard the music in my mind from some distant memory, and I began to sing to the Lord. "I surrender all, all to thee my precious Savior, I surrender all." Worship was all I could do at the moment; it was all I had left. Again, I wept cleansing tears. My only hope for peace was to trust God's will. His presence filled the air, into my lungs, filled my wounded soul but most importantly, it filled the cracks of my broken heart.

∴

The song in our heart reflects the state of our mind. I accepted my future; I accepted no matter the outcome God would be faithful. I believed His word and promises, I knew it would not make sense to the human or social norms. Hebrews 4:16, Let us then approach God's throne of grace with confidence, so that we may receive mercy and find grace to help us in our time of need.

Equipped.

Christmas was around the corner, but we had not decorated a thing. I could not bring myself to hang a wreath or a stocking. The tree was still boxed up in the attic. Presents were not bought, no letters had been written to Santa, no plans of celebrations or Christmas classic movies were watched. Christmas was on pause. It was deeper than the red and green decor, the spirit of Christmas was on pause too. Like Pastor Lonnie from that sermon I was thinking about the work of the cross and death and grief and suffering.

Officer Kurt was back from the Border Patrol duty safe and sound. I prayed so hard for him while deployed and felt relieved when he messaged me that he was back in town. We were ready for an answer. I had paid my retainer in full with donations and garage sales. Checking as many boxes off my list to prepare as best I could.

Every night I have made it a practice to find the good in the day. Without fail, as I lay in bed waiting for the melatonin to kick in, things to be grateful for would pop up. There was a bumper sticker I saw today that read, "You can do hard things, just not with my bumper." I laughed so hard I snorted.

The creator of that car sticker had no idea.

God was all around us, providing financially and giving us just what we needed for the day. He never stopped being present. I was just more intentionally seeking out hope. Searching for small miracles and treasures for my soul from God. Talking to him continuously, moment to moment. I could look back at how far I've come. Flipping through the pages of my journal, you can see a difference. You don't even have to read it to see the change in handwriting, the shift in tone, the changes in perspective. Pages of prayers, letters to David, and dreams.

In my notebook, I wrote the word equipped. Here I am still fighting the good fight. I remember thinking I couldn't make it to the end of the week.

The Lord gave me a memory. It felt like a dream, but it was a real flashback from twelve years ago. A woman gave her testimony at our church, where we were the youth ministers. Brooklynn was four months old. I almost didn't attend because it was during her nursing schedule. We were studying the "Be-Attitudes." I had asked God to help me with meekness. The woman wore a pale pink dress suit. Her hair was short, and I remember thinking I might cut mine like hers to curl under, framing my face. This guest speaker was all the buzz around the church; everyone described her testimony as powerful. The room grew intensely still, captivated by her story of great faith. She began to tell us the hardships she and her family had overcome. She attested that her every breath depended on the Lord during those dark days.

I wasn't prepared for what she shared next, but I could close my eyes right now and feel her words. Her husband had accidentally backed over their young son in their driveway, and he passed away. Listening to her share so openly, every eye was weeping and every heartbreaking for the pain she endured. The husband, stricken with grief six months later, lost his battle of depression and took his own life. Her transparency about how she coped with God's help inspired us all.

What stood out besides her evident faith was the love that remained for her husband, how much she missed him desperately. She grieved him deeply. There was no anger and resentment for his mistakes, but a firm resolve to not let the enemy win. We could not fathom such pain because it was not our burden to bear, but she stood as a witness to the strength and power of God who carried her through it. This is what it looks like to be comforted by the Lord in a supernatural, beyond understanding way.

My hormones were just a mess. With my infant swaddled tightly in my arms, her blanket was damp from my tears. This same baby would later be the one to witness a tragic accident and share the experience of perhaps the greatest pain I might ever know. This memory was preserved like amber in the chaos of my mind. I talked to God about this unexpected recall. It gave me peace. As painful as it is to think the accident might always be a part of my and David's journey, it reaffirmed that nothing is a surprise to God.

Three months have passed, and this memory only solidified the need to pursue healing with everything I could muster. There was still a faint whisper I might end up like the husband. I lay there filled with emotions in both awe and wonder because this revelation was so big, but there was zero anxiety. Another entry for the notebook dated December 12, 2016, is another miracle to add to the growing list of mercies and miracles. *What's my One Word for 2017? Hope? Believe? Trust? This year might need three, don't give up.*

The day before the Grand Jury, I had Professional Development training for the math department in Dallas. We collaborated on best practices and planned how to best support our struggling students for the next semester. I tried to ignore that I was planning a semester I might not participate in. The Grand Jury would be meeting the next day.

When we started wrapping up, my colleagues were headed for dinner, and I would head back home.

"I just want all of you to know how much I appreciate your love and support through this whole ordeal. Please pray for us all tomorrow. We think everything will be okay. I just don't know what okay really means. But thank you." In the middle school math department, a group of God-sent team members moved in and surrounded me with a group hug.

On a stretch of highway, 45 minutes from home, I realized all this time waiting led to tomorrow.

LEFT TURN, LIFE UNIMAGINED

Coordinating our four children to each be with friends was less angst than what to wear for court. I had talked with our closest friends, and everyone had a place to go, a bag packed, and each family had a plan to distract our kids with an activity. This allowed Keith and my mom to just focus on me. I prepared for the worst-case scenario.

"Honey, here is a list of names and phone numbers of who will have the kids after school, so you don't have to worry." I was going over things with Keith, he put his hand on mine and his eyes filled with worry. "Mom will be here in the morning to sit with us until we know the jury's decision. If the lawyer calls and I need to get to the courthouse, Mom will help you." I am pretty sure all he heard was the blah blah blah... But when I said *post bond*, something clicked, and he was shell-shocked.

It hit him. The look on his face read he had not mentally prepared for this day. He had put it aside, and aside, and aside until here we are.

"Don't worry, mom will be there with you to help you bond me out."

"Out," as in behind the wooden door of a courtroom where I would be taken with an officer and input into the system, the fingerprints-the whole process and have a decision trial or take a plea bargain to avoid a very long emotionally draining process and thousands of dollars we didn't have.

"They will take me back for processing in a separate place, and I will be safe. It's called a walk-through."

In almost seventeen years of doing life with this man, I've only seen his lip-quiver twice. It finally hit him what might happen. His body said tag you're it, he tapped out. I was unusually calm, given what might happen. I let him be emotional, and I swallowed back the fear and tears. I don't know if I disconnected emotionally or God gave me supernatural peace, but I was ready.

JEN EIKENHORST

⁂

When I think about this moment it doesn't feel like it was me. If you asked me how I did it, I can't give you an answer other than the Lord was our strength. It was not of my power but the beautiful gift of grace. Proverbs 31:25, She is clothed with strength and dignity; she can laugh at the days to come.

Saving grace.

This will be the last meeting before this group of jurors were dismissed of their commitment to serve our county. I cannot imagine the responsibility. There is a time I would have happily served on something like that. Blind faith in our justice system. It has its flaws, but I believe justice prevails.

When your freedom is on the line, having faith is an entirely different story. Saying you trust a system that you know is broken but trusting it anyway is easier said than done.

Just after 8 a.m., Mr. Strawn was headed into the courtroom. I was rendered useless waiting by my phone, waiting to hear if I was needed to answer the jury's questions. I decided to put on my nicest denim jeans and a black floral blouse. We waited. No desire for small talk. Mom, Keith, and I just sat around the kitchen counter, staring at my phone.

10:06 a.m. I was standing to stretch my legs just about to walk the dogs when the phone rang. Strawn Cell popped up on the caller I.D.

I looked at them in shock before sliding over the screen to answer the call. We gasped at the sound of the ring. Holding back her fear, my mom motioned that maybe you should go upstairs where it is quiet. I made it to the top of our staircase and sank to the floor.

"Yes, sir, do I need to come down?" *Just breathe, is what I told myself.*

"Hello, is this Jenna? My name is Steven Munich, District Attorney. I am using Strawn's phone here to let you know the county will not be pressing charges." He said it so matter of fact.

"The Grand Jury just unanimously voted a No Bill decision in your case. The No Bill means dismissed. They wanted me to call you, something I don't normally do, but I made an exception with their request. They wanted you to know without waiting until the end of the day. They all wish you a very Merry Christmas, and they want you to find peace."

I couldn't even speak.

I am not sure my "thank you" was even intelligible. Dear God, I hope I said thank you and Merry Christmas to you as well, but I was so stunned. We hung up, and I could not recount what was said other than No Bill and Merry Christmas.

Thank you, God, thank you for your mercies. Thank you, God! Thank you; I don't deserve your goodness but thank you. I praise you, God. I can't believe it.

I came down the stairs crying so hard I stumbled the last three to four steps. I am pretty sure Keith and mom didn't breathe until I could utter the words, "It's over, no charges, that was the District Attorney who called." My mom lowered her head in her hands and released three months of worry and anxiety with grateful tears. Her knees buckled and the kitchen counter held her weight so that she didn't fall. She had stayed strong, at least in front of me, but her body let it go, and it all came pouring out. "Oh, thank God," I heard her say over and over.

It wasn't a celebration with tears and sighs of relief. It was a deep, slow exhale. The text with the news went out to the prayer chain, "No bill, it's over, the Grand Jury wanted me to know early. We don't need to meet at the square for prayer. It's done. Thank you, a million times, over for your support!"

Dear David,

I alone secretly thought of David's family while Keith and Mom began to spread the good news. There was hugging and crying, but I thought of them. I tried to imagine their faces and their tears. Were they accepting of this decision? How did they feel? I wished I could tell them that just because a judge and jury and District Attorney had pardoned me, it wasn't over in my heart. Their grief was still very tender, and it mattered to me.

The day returned to just a Wednesday. One of my mom's ways of showing love and appreciation is to bake. We delivered handmade pies to the sheriff's office, Dr. Knox, and Mr. Strawn's office was the last stop. It was brighter than when I had first visited a little over a month ago. It was festive with the Christmas spirit. He greeted me with a smile, "Justice won today." His wife was just as happy with the news, and I got my hug.

I passed out hugs to everyone in the office. The small hateful voice chastised me about celebrating as the excitement wound down. Everyone around me saw my smile and my eyes glistened with relief but I heard a voice in my head, "That b!-—got away with murder." I winced briefly like bad indigestion bubbled up. The battle of the mind wasn't over, but I put it in a box, stuck it on the shelf and said, "I'll get to you later."

All the plans I had so carefully made to divide the kids to our various friends while we handled my court stuff were canceled. I wanted them home with me. I wanted to smell them and snuggle them as close to my heart as possible. I felt as if I had a new appreciation for everything, especially my faith, family, and friends.

I pulled up in the carline; the teacher with the walkie-talkie called for Hazel to be released. "Hey, how are you?" A teacher attendant asked me. It had been a while since I did the school pick-up. "I'm doing okay. We're doing better. I am really grateful.

Really very grateful." Hazel appeared from the school doors, her backpack as big as her body, and her face shown with joy seeing me.

"Momma, you are here? I thought I was going home with someone else."

"Yes, baby, I am!" My heart was full of hope like mortar for the cracks in my still broken heart. We would be okay. Grief and joy walked hand in hand. I had many things to learn, restore, and surrender, but I hoped my heart would heal in time. There was more life to live. Someday I hope my journey will help someone else.

Knowing the Grand Jury decision freed up energy that had been devoted just to worry. It was time for Christmas, binge watch all the holiday classics, cookie decorating, presents to buy, and fight with everything in me to make this pain have a purpose. This was grace, what the cross stands for. I will not squander it. This horrible thing that has happened caused many to draw closer to the Lord, that is good. My faith is stronger, my hope restored, and I humbly embrace forgiveness as a living testimony.

Dear David,

I will never understand why this happened to you or me, but I will never forget. I will honor your life with the rest of the time I am blessed with on earth. I will smile when I see sailboats because I know you love them. Maybe even sail someday. I will help people make better decisions on the road to prevent more accidents and share how your life changed mine. You taught me that life is short and precious. To live it. Thank you for that. You taught me that I shouldn't have opinions on everything that doesn't concern me. My energy should be placed in joy and what brings me joy and not worry, anger, or resentment. Your death made me seek out my faith on a deeper, more personal level. I see and feel Jesus more intimately through this grief. It taught me more than words can express. This pain helped me realize that there is beauty amongst the ashes. There is beauty in the process of pain. Thank you, David, for the lessons this process taught me. I am sorry it happened in this way, but I am grateful I'm learning. Your memory will always be a part of me, David. I will not let your death be in vain. I will help others; I will educate others about the dangers. I will not spread more pain, I will not grow bitter, I will live life to honor yours as best I can.

Always,

Jenna

I created a secret prayer group on Facebook. I asked these women to commit to praying with me and for me, to pray when I couldn't, and they upheld me. Faithful, beautiful souls. Thank you to each of you.

Dear God,

Thank you for hope being restored. Thank you for how my heart grew. Thank you for listening to me even when I didn't feel you. Thank you for the grace, your endless grace. Thank you that just when hope would begin to fade, you sent a sign that carried me until the next day. I will seek you in this situation. I believe you will heal my broken heart. I will tell the hurting that they are not alone, and that suffering does not last forever. I will serve you all my life, Lord. Tell me where to go and I will go. Tell what to say and how to pray and for whom and I will obey. Send me. Let my life honor David and honor you in all that I do. I honor you, Lord. I lay down my shame, I lay down my guilt, I lay down the lies of unworthiness. You are my strength. Help me to let go and let you lead. Help me to forgive myself and trust you as the author of my life.

In Jesus' precious name, Amen

For David

We never met but for a sacred brief moment.

Tragic.

Honored to hold your hand, filled with disbelief,

Confused.

Declared healing, spoken prayer, hoped for relief,

JEN EIKENHORST

Waited.
Our souls entangled and swept like wind and leaf,
Taken.
You couldn't stay, my head and heart filled with grief,
Crushed.
I'm so sorry please forgive me, repeat,
Defeat.
I looked for hope and peace and exposed the true thief,
Understanding.
Truth led me to follow Jesus' footsteps along the tranquil seif,
Guided.
Looked to heaven where the rolling sea meets the reef,
Glory.
Covered in grace, filled with joy, purpose restored,
Belief.

Salvation

Friends, I will say this again, please hear me, I breathe and walk in freedom in Christ alone. I made a decision to accept Jesus as my Lord and Savior and because of that choice nothing is wasted, not even heartache. Especially heartache. You may wonder why I came to know the Lord the way that I did. I was curious too. When I was thirty, God gave me my answer. I was talking to my uncle (my dad's brother). We have not had much interaction with him because my uncle struggles with addiction. His vice has cost him, greatly. But, he loves the Lord with his whole heart. When he has spent time in prison, he gets sober and he is used for the Kingdom of God.

On this phone call he begins to weep and praise God. I tried to comfort him and he corrected me. He is overjoyed that I love the Lord. He tells me that my belief has increased his faith, encouraged him, and an answer to prayer. I felt the presence of the Lord come over me as he spoke. When I was a baby, swaddled and laying in a playpen napping, my Uncle Kim came and laid his hand on my tiny back. He said he could still remember his hand covering my whole little back. He prayed for my salvation. That I would come to know the Lord in a deep and personal way. He prayed that my life would be used to glorify the Lord and be a witness to my mom and dad. Hallelujah! I was weeping covered in goosebumps and I knew this was a revelation from the Lord.

There is power in standing the gap in faithful prayer, God is there for it. He used this man who suffered much of his own doing. Addiction. Prison. Failed marriage. Broken. But used in a mighty way for the salvation of others and I am eternally grateful.

If you do not know Jesus as your personal Lord and Savior, I implore you to get curious. Cry out and ask him to speak to you. Literally say, "Lord, are you there?" "Jesus, are you real?" This audacious faith is for everyone, Jesus is waiting. He knows you and loves you more than you can imagine. Ask him to reveal himself. Get to know him through prayer (conversation) and reading his scriptures. Then ask him to be Lord of your life. Confess your sin and ask for healing and forgiveness. You will embark on the greatest journey you could ever imagine. Welcome to the family. Amen.

Dear Lord, I feel something in my heart, is that you? I want to know more about you. I acknowledge I can't do this on my own. I surrender my life to your will. Please, forgive me of my sins, help me to heal, help me to turn from them. I want you to come into my heart and into my life as my Lord and Savior. In Jesus' name, Amen.

Scripture references: Matthew 6:9-13 and Romans 10:9-10

Afterword

What happened next? It was all sunshine and roses, hardly the truth. All jokes aside, the Lord continued to heal my broken heart, in time. We moved away from the town that harbored many painful memories besides the incredible people who carried us during the accident. Leaving them felt like a blooming branch broke off. We were officially pruned and God did all but sent a burning flame in the sky that led us to our next assignment. Once again, we faced many trials, including BIG "T" and little "t" traumas. Unfortunately we can not escape hardships of this life but we learned through the experience of the accident that God will provide hope for whatever may come. He wastes nothing, our testimony will encourage others if we allow him to work through us.

What kept us going? God provided miracles and restored all that was lost after the accident including a beautiful family dining table. It isn't Italian but it is loved just the same. God answered my prayer, and I met more C.A.D.I.s. I was able to find a community. I have devoted my life's work to advocating for accident prevention and recovery. The Lord opened doors to share on incredible platforms such as with The New Yorker journalist Alice Gregory, What Was That Like Podcast (Ep 1), and Red Table Talk with Jada Pinkett-Smith (Ep 99). With encouragement from friends and a strong nudge from the Lord, I launched the Accidental Hope Podcast that shares stories of hope after an accident with fatality worldwide. I am still recovering from my accident.

Friends, if you hold bitterness or unforgiveness in your heart, please lay it down today. Write a letter to the one who hurt you, send it or burn it. Watch the wind scatter the ashes and cry. While you weep, pray. Praise the Lord for what you learned and how you grew, thank God you are stronger. Tell the devil he can't win. Your story belongs to God and pray for the soul of the letter recipient. That is beautiful. If you hurt someone, confess it. Take a sharpie and write it on a stone and toss that rock in a river. The water (like the living water) will wash it away. Your identity is in Christ alone, not the choices you've made. How you change and learn and grow develops your character, your testimony, and that is equally as beautiful.

    I still pray daily for David's family, and I live my life hopefully honoring his memory. Through therapy, sharing my experience, and helping others, my outlook on life has regained health. I breathe easier and laugh without guilt. I know who God says I am, and his voice drowns out the intrusive thoughts that tormented me for a season. I battle anxiety to this day but I have been given tools to combat and treat the symptoms. I've learned how to protect my peace. There is hope in living a full life after tragedy; I am walking proof. I remain eternally grateful to the Lord, my supportive family, and the beautiful souls I call friends. To learn more about the work, I am committed to visit, www.accidentalhope.com

Acknowledgement

I want to acknowledge the sacrifice of my family that supported me during the four-year process to write this book. Thank you, and I love you! I had the help of many friends that edited and gave vital opinions to see this project birthed. The following are not limited to just these amazing selfless friends, so I thank you if you helped in any way. Dr. John Knox, Elizabeth Oates (Collab Conference for Writers), Lana Jackson-Brown, Stephanie Snyder, Ralinda Fenton, Allison Buras, Amy Taylor, Michelle Bentham, Anna Mitchael, David Peters, Maryann Gray and the Left Turn book launch team.

About the Author

Jennifer Eikenhorst is a wife, mom of 4, math teacher and podcast host for Accidental Hope Podcast. Her passion when not helping students succeed in math is advocating for accident prevention and serious accident recovery. Jennifer is a C.A.D.I. (Causing Accidental Death or Injury) and shares her journey of healing to help others. Jennifer was featured on Red Table Talk sharing her story.

Read more at https://accidentalhope.com/.